EUROPEAN FOOD AID POLICY

European Food Aid Policy

JOHN CATHIE

Agricultural Economics Unit/Department of Land Economy
University of Cambridge

Ashgate

Aldershot • Brookfield USA • Singapore • Sydney

Published by
Ashgate Publishing Limited
Gower House
Croft Road
Aldershot
Hants GU11 3HR
England

Ashgate Publishing Company
Old Post Road
Brookfield
Vermont 05036
USA

British Library Cataloguing in Publication Data

Cathie, John
   European food aid policy
   1.Food relief - Developing countries 2.Economic assistance,
   European - Developing countries 3.Agriculture and state -
   European Union countries
   I.Title
   338.1'81'0917124

Library of Congress Catalog Card Number: 97-70895

ISBN 1 85972 599 6

Printed and bound by Athenaeum Press, Ltd.,
Gateshead, Tyne & Wear.

Contents

Figures and tables

Preface

Over the many years that I have studied food aid and food security problems, issues and policies, many individuals and organisations have given freely of encouragement, criticism and advice. I am particularly indebted to I M Sturgess, Director of the Agricultural Economics Unit, and Professor M Grant, both of the Department of Land Economy for their support for this study.

John Cathie

Abbreviations and acronyms

ACP	African, Caribbean and Pacific group of seventy countries, signatories of the EU Lome Convention
ADB	Africa Development Bank
ASI	International Solidarity Association, French acronym for NGO
CAP	Common Agricultural Policy of the EU
CCC	Commodity Credit Corporation of the US Department of Agriculture
CCP	Committee in Commodity Problems (FAO)
CEEC	Central and Eastern European Countries
CSD	Committee on Surplus Disposal (FAO)
CUP	Customs Union Policy of the EU
DAC	Development Assistance Committee (OECD)
DG	Directorate General of the European Union
ECHO	European Community Humanitarian Office
ECU	European Currency Unit
EDF	European Development Fund
EFTA	European Free Trade Area
EU/EC/EEC	European Union (also known prior to the Maastricht Treaty as EC, Economic Community, EEC, European Economic Community)
ERP	European Recovery Programme (Marshall Plan)
FAC	Food Aid Convention (of the International Wheat Agreements)

FAO	Food and Agricultural Organisation of United Nations
FFHC	Freedom from Hunger Campaign of the FAO
FSR	Former Soviet Republics
GATT	General Agreement on Tariffs and Trade (now known as the WTO)
GIEWS	Global Information and Early Warning System of FAO
GSP	Generalised System of Preferences
IBRD	International Bank for Reconstruction and Development (World Bank)
ICRC	International Committee of the Red Cross
IFAD	International Fund for Agricultural Development
IEFR	International Emergency Food Reserve of the WFP
IMF	International Monetary Fund
INTERFAIS	International Food Aid Information System of WFP
IWA	International Wheat Agreement(s)
IWC	International Wheat Council
LRCS	League of Red Cross (Red Crescent) Societies
NDDB	National Dairy Development Board (Operation Flood India)
MSF	Medecins sans Frontiéres (French NGO)
NGO	Non-governmental Organisations (also known as NGDO, non-governmental development organisations and NGAOs non-governmental aid organisations)
NOHA	Network on Humanitarian Assistance
ODA	Official Development Assistance
ODA	Overseas Development Administration of the UK
OECD	Organisation for Economic Co-operation and Development
OJ	Official Journal of the EU
PL 480	Public Law 480, United States Food Aid Programme
SADCC	Southern African Development Co-ordination Conference
SADC	Southern African Development Community (successor to SADCC)
SMP	Skimmed milk powder
UMRs	Usual Marketing Requirements
UNCTAD	The United Nations Conference on Trade and Development
UNHCR	United Nations High Commission for Refugees
UNRWA	United National Relief and Works Agency (Palestine Refugees)

USDA	United States Department of Agriculture
USAID	United States Agency for International Development
WB	World Bank
WFC	World Food Council
WFC	World Food Conference (1974)
WFP	World Food Programme of the United Nations
WTO	World Trade Organisation (successor to GATT)

Introduction

Over the last thirty years the food aid policy that has emerged in Europe and associated with the European Union (EU)1, is a part of the European economic and political integration process that emerged after the Second World War. Food aid has come to play a prominent role as one of the few community-wide economic aid policies that has a distinctive European character and identity and is operated on behalf of the union as a whole by the Commission and the Council of Ministers as a coherent policy, separate from that operated by the member states in their own food aid projects, programmes, humanitarian, emergency and relief operations.

While the Community has a common trade and agricultural policy which has developed over the past thirty-six years, other areas of common policy, such as monetary, fiscal, exchange rate, foreign and defence spheres have emerged in an erratic and often fragmented form and not embracing all the members of the European community. The process of economic and political integration has gone through many different stages over the past three and a half decades, where common policies and agreement have resulted in a kind of convergence of direction and singular aim and objectives. This process has not of course been linear and free from dispute, delays and direction changes, as compromise has narrowed the range of options for the nation states to converge their economic, social and political structures and policies.

The emergence of a single European food aid policy has a significance that goes beyond the monetary value of the food given by the Union to developing countries for developmental and humanitarian purposes. Since

1

in 1989, for example, food aid from the European Union represented some 22% of its overseas development assistance. The Community now contributes more than half of the total food aid given from Europe to the third world and transitional economies. Food aid policy and programmes have gradually become a singular European policy issue, rather than being merely the sum of fifteen different national food aid policies. In 1991 Community Action was over 60% of total European food aid.

European food aid has a significance for the Community as a whole as it provides an increasingly high profile role for the Commission to operate a single developmental and humanitarian policy towards the non-European world as one other facet of its trade, aid and external relations policy. Food aid policy has become de-nationalised over the last thirty years and has gradually been subsumed into a European Union single policy, this has implications for other areas of national policy that the Commission and the European parliament would wish to aspire to. A European food aid policy has emerged as a subset of a wider European development aid policy where the Commission has gradually gained more authority for a single European policy. This work traces the origins and the growth of a European food aid policy from its establishment in the late 1960s to the present time.

After the United States of America, the European Union is the second largest donor of world food aid and has held this position since the mid-1970s. The EU provides, in the 1990s, some 25% of world food aid resources for developmental and humanitarian purposes, to 120 different recipient countries. The use of commodities surplus to world effective demand as food aid, arose as a consequence of technological induced productivity increases in agricultural production and government price and intervention support for the agricultural sector. Food aid policy was a secondary outcome of agricultural protection and the United States pioneered the use of agricultural surpluses for developmental and relief purposes from the Marshall plan of the 1940s until the mid-1960s, world food aid policy was essentially an American affair until the emergence of a UN multilateral system of food aid donations in the 1960s.

The European involvement with food aid as a donor, was a direct outcome of an American request that the burden of the costs of world food aid should be shared amongst rich country agricultural producers and consumers and that the era of surplus disposal of agricultural

2

commodities, at least from the United States standpoint, as 'bread basket for the world', was to end. Chapter One examines the origins of the European food aid programme in 1968, in the context of the International Wheat Agreement of 1967 and the establishment of the Food Aid Convention. European Union food aid policy and the food aid policies of the nation states of Europe were a direct consequence of the question of the burden-sharing of world food aid supplies which had been raised by the United States in the 1960s.

The existence of a food aid policy and programme was a direct outcome of agricultural protection in the world cereals market which had created capacity and output well in excess of world effective demand for nearly three decades since the 1940s. European involvement with food aid began in a reluctant and half-hearted way, with her burden-sharing obligations being met in the main through the UN multilateral food aid agency the World Food Programme and through donations to the International Red Cross agencies. A distinctive EU food aid policy began to emerge in the mid-1970s, as did a distinctive European developmental, trade and aid policy towards selective developing countries.

Chapter Two considers the EU food aid policy since 1968 tracing its growth and its relationship to the Food Aid Convention of the International Wheat Agreements and the evolution of the EU cereals programme food aid. During the decade of the 1970s, the EU response to the world food crisis proved a turning point for its food aid policy as the Union established a greater share of European food aid and began to formulate a Union-wide policy. Chapter Two considers the relationship between the Community food aid programme and the fifteen different national food aid programmes of the member states of the Union.

Over nearly three decades, European food aid has become less concerned with surplus disposal and agricultural trade although the issue of the relationship of the Common Agricultural Policy and cereals food aid remains inextricably connected through the Food Aid Convention and the rules of the principles of surplus disposal which were designed to prevent cereals export dumping. Chapter Three examines the issue of the surplus disposal of European cereals and the growing European trade in cereals.

The formulation and management of European food aid policy and programmes is considered in Chapter Four. The world food crisis of the

1970s, the African food crisis of the mid-1980s and the collapse of the Soviet Union in the late 1980s provided defining external events that have shaped European aid and food aid policies and have brought the Union and particularly the Commission of the Union to formulate a proactive Union policy in response to these events, either through proposing a distinctive European-wide policy, or arguing for the co-ordination of the policies of the member states. The balance between the authority of the Commission for the formation and management of policy and that of the Council of Development Ministers is a theme that has preoccupied food aid matters throughout the existence of the programme. The Commission has gradually become the singular focus for both the formulation and management of a European food aid policy, since its own programme has become larger than the combined national member state programmes.

European food aid policy has a multilateral character which has been the result of its close association with the World Food Programme and the Food and Agricultural Organisation of the United Nations. Chapter Five traces the influence and the elements of multilateralism within European food aid as well as examining the growth of the non-governmental organisations' relationship as receivers of EU food as resources for their charitable projects and programmes in the Third World.

Chapter Six looks at some of the issues relating to the effectiveness of European food aid as a development resource, as well as the distribution of the resource to developing countries. While cereals food aid has been the major commodity in volume terms, surplus milk powder and butteroil have in value terms been a significant share of European food aid from the 1970s and 1980s. The European Union funds the world's largest rural development programme, Operation Flood in India with surplus skimmed milk powder and butteroil from the food aid programme. The effects of this twenty-five-year-old rural development Programme are also considered in Chapter Six, as is the role of funds (counterpart funds) raised from the sales of food aid in developing countries on the budget of the recipient countries.

A European food aid programme started as a means of using surplus agricultural commodities for the economic development and emergency relief in developing countries. As the programme has evolved over time it has responded to outside obligations such as the Food Aid Convention; it has also been a direct response to the world food crisis, the African food crisis and to the more recent food import requirements of the former Soviet Union and Eastern European countries.

European food aid policy has broadened its scope to embrace a wider food strategy approach to economic development, which includes elements of multilateral food aid policy together with a regional emphasis with regard to food security objectives. The Union has moved from a narrow approach to disposing of unwanted surplus agricultural commodities for development, to formulating a broader approach that emphasises the importance of trade in agricultural commodities as a means of promoting food security and agricultural development in the Third World. The Community, in drawing on its own experience with agricultural and agricultural objectives in the Common Agricultural Policy, promotes policies within its food aid and food security programmes that encourage government interventions in agriculture to try to attain production and consumption objectives within developing countries and within regions of the developing world. This policy emphasis contrasts with that proposed by the Bretton Woods Institutions who favour food security through markets and competition. The EU in its structural adjustment emphasis of its aid programmes in the 1990s is coming closer to those structural adjustment and conditionality policies advocated by the World Bank and the International Monetary Fund, particularly with regard to the financial impact of the sales of surplus commodities for revenue raising purposes by recipients in developing countries.

European food aid has moved from being an adjunct of its agricultural trade policy to that of being a part of a wider aid policy for the Union as a whole. A distinctive EU food aid approach has emerged as the changing balance of authority between the Union and the member states for the formulation of policy has moved in favour of the Commission. European food aid policy has become part of a broader approach by the Commission to acquire a presence in areas of policy over and above national member states policies where development objectives and humanitarian objectives merge into foreign policy. These developments promoted by the Commission in and with food aid policy over two and a half decades, illustrate the convergence of foreign policy objectives within the Union. Food aid may have provided a prototype of a European-wide common policy towards one aspect of external relations and foreign affairs that is less controversial for member states to relinquish than other areas of foreign policy may prove to be.

Note

1 The European integration process adopted in the Maastricht Treaty the name 'European Union', as a replacement for previous names and acronyms. EU, EEC, Economic Community are used as synonyms in this work.

1 The background to and the establishment of the European food aid programme

1.1 The origins of European food aid and world food aid policy: European involvement with emerging food aid policies 1940-1962

The European experience with food as a form of aid began during the Second World War when the United States of America donated agricultural commodities in support of the allies' war effort, under the lend-lease programme. The US had provided food relief during the first war and the period after, especially to Belgium and France, to the value of $5.2 billion (Surface and Bland, 1932). This agricultural commodity aid was extended under the European Recovery Programme (the Marshall Plan) from 1945 until 1949. In 1941 lend-lease provided over $6 billion in agricultural commodities (mainly cereals) to sixteen European allies (Wallerstein, 1980). From 1945 agricultural commodities to Europe under US government support increased from 56 million bushels and peaked at 505 million bushels in 1949 (Cathie, 1982).

The European Recovery Programme was the largest food aid programme in volume and value terms that the world has yet known and was mainly given in the form of grants. American generosity provided the basis for European-wide economic recovery with the Marshall plan and half of this aid was in the form of food grants (Bairoch, 1975). From 1948 until 1952 saw substantial food aid flows to the United Kingdom, France, Italy, West Germany and Greece who received the lion's share of the aid (Adams, 1968). Other European countries, most notably the

Netherlands, who had experienced famine towards the end of the war were beneficiaries of food grants under the Marshall Plan. All European countries had experienced food rationing and food shortages as a consequence of the war.

American food aid had provided the basis for gradual economic recovery and, perhaps more importantly, the prevention of famine in parts of Europe and the alleviation of food shortages. American aid to European recovery lasted until the early 1950s and demonstrated that food surpluses could contribute to reconstruction and could help provide the basis for stability and economic growth. The effects of the Marshall Plan and the food aid component have generally been accepted as having made a major and significant contribution to post war European economic recovery. It was as a receiver rather than a giver that Europe first experienced food aid, in the post war years, and that experience has influenced a number of countries, most notably the Netherlands in its favourable attitude towards food aid and its potential as a resource for economic development (WFP Government of Netherlands Seminar on Food Aid, 1983). The benefits of food aid to Europe were considered as a once and for all one-off programme, of commodity transfers contributing to economic and social stability as well as economic growth.

Europe and Japan both received substantial volumes of food aid from the United States after the second world war as a major part of America's real resource contribution to building a liberal economic order. Food aid to most of these countries was however a relatively short-term affair and was gradually phased out when economic stability and recovery became apparent in the 1950s. However, transfers of food aid under American programmes to countries such as Greece, Spain, Yugoslavia continued throughout the 1960s and 1970s and, in the case of the former Yugoslavia, up until that country's demise in the 1990s.

The period of the early 1950s saw the establishment of a permanent US food aid programme with Public Law 480 in 1954. This programme was to provide food aid as a development contribution for the emerging post colonial less developed countries. It was one of the components of American Foreign Policy, the other components being military and financial aid for economic development. Lend-lease and the Marshall Plan had increased the markets for United States agricultural exports (albeit paid for by the American taxpayer) in the immediate post war period and its agricultural output far exceeded domestic and world effective demand.

Government price supports for agriculture taken together with large holdings of food stocks, particularly cereals and the productivity changes from the application of technology to agriculture resulted in the development of food aid policy and programmes. This policy was designed as much to help the recipients of the aid as it was designed to relieve the surplus overhang of output increases well in excess of the capacity of markets to absorb these products at given world prices. The inconvertibility of currencies was also a major restraint on the purchase of American Farm Products; this situation prevailed throughout the 1950s.

Almost from its inception in 1954 PL 480 ran into difficulties, since this aid programme was seen as a disguised means of export dumping and therefore an unfair means of competition in agricultural trade, particularly from export competitors who were unable to develop their agricultural markets using the financial resources that were available from the American taxpayer to fund the recipients of PL 480. It was recognised from its inception that PL 480 had the potential to do harm to the international agricultural trading system (as much as it might benefit recipients of food), and therefore also do harm to the newly established general trading system under the General Agreement on Tariffs and Trade (GATT). Although agricultural trade was in effect exempt from these GATT rules until the Uruguay Round successfully incorporated agriculture into the rules of its successor, the World Trade Organisation of the 1990s.

The capacity of food aid or surplus disposal of agricultural commodities to disrupt markets for competitor agricultural exporters, was recognised in the attempts to monitor trade by the Committee on Commodity Problems (CCP) of the Food and Agricultural Organisation (FAO) of the United Nations and particularly by a Washington-based sub-committee which was concerned with establishing the "rules of the game" with regard to surplus disposal. The principles of surplus disposal were formulated in 1954 to try to safeguard commercial agricultural transactions against displacement by dumping practices and by concessional sales of food aid. The consultative Sub-Committee on Surplus Disposal (CSD) had as its terms of reference 'that the disposal of surpluses be made without harmful interference with the normal patterns of production and international trade' (FAO, 1954 and 1972). Members

9

of the working party were Argentina, Egypt, France, India, the Netherlands, New Zealand, the UK and the USA. The Committee has met monthly since 1954 to consider the interests of third party exporting countries by discussing in advance the surplus disposal agreements between donors and recipients of food aid.

The deliberations of the CSD over the years have refined these principles into three concepts: additionality, orderly disposal and voluntary consultation. Additionality attempted to determine the conditions of surplus disposal of agricultural commodities, such that they would be additional to normal commercial sales in recipient countries. In practice the precise circumstances of the additionality principle have been difficult to determine and at best it has operated as a partial safeguard for third party interests. Both orderly disposal of agricultural stocks and voluntary consultation amongst members to the agreement of surplus disposal principles did provide some restraint on blatant dumping practices. However the potential for food aid as a source of unfair competition was moderated not eliminated (see Cathie, 1982, Chapter Three).

The principles of surplus disposal were later reformulated and Usual Marketing Requirements (UMRs) were added to give more precision and practical definition to its principles. The CSD recognised in 1968 that additionality was very difficult to define in practical terms because it was almost impossible to determine how much of a particular food commodity a country would have imported in the absence of a transaction on special aid terms (see Cathie 1982 for a further discussion of this concept).

While the European Community of the Customs Union was not to be established until the Treaty of Rome of 1958 and the Common Agricultural policy of 1962, some individual European states' interests were represented on the Committee of Surplus Disposal, namely France, the Netherlands and the United Kingdom, and the 'European Interest' was equal to that of the representation from developing countries. France had made ad hoc food aid contributions in its bilateral food aid programmes in the 1950s, while the United Kingdom and the Netherlands had not established bilateral food aid programmes.

The food aid policy established in the 1950s was largely an American affair and world food aid policy was in effect determined by the United States agricultural trade and aid objectives. Although European countries and European interests were represented in the initial framework, that of the principles of surplus disposal, which sought to moderate what was a potential if not actual interference with international agricultural trade and the competitive process. The principles of surplus disposal pre-date the European Customs Union and the Common Agricultural Policy, nevertheless three future European Union countries were represented on the Committee and no doubt contributed to the arrangements and the establishment of these less than perfect rules of the game that sought to moderate surplus disposals in their most harmful form. From its very inception food aid policy, with the exception of the European Recovery Programme (the Marshall Plan), was to provide a source of contention as a development aid transfer because of its affects on competition in international agricultural trade and because the self-interest of the donor country, the United States was expanding its own international markets and agricultural exports. From 1954 until the late 1970s the US share of world agricultural trade increased from 25% of that trade to as much as 70% (Cathie, 1985). Concessional sales (Food Aid) of US farm products during the 1950s and 1960s comprised an average of 30% over the period and in the late 1950s as much as 40% of American farm sales (Cathie, 1989).

The effects of concessional sales of food aid on international agricultural competition were the major concern that emerged in the 1960s and produced pressure for the moderation of export sales by attempting to tighten the international voluntary agreement operated by the Sub-Committee on surplus disposals. The mechanism of the CSD was, however, an inadequate instrument to oversee international agricultural competition, and its rules were of the most rudimentary kind which at best provided a forum for complaint with regard to the most blatant forms of export dumping. The CSD principles were not designed to prevent concessional sales of food aid, or the development of American agricultural export markets.

The creation of markets for American farm produce in Europe and the Far East during the 1950s and 1960s attests to the beneficial transition of countries as concessional sales recipients to commercial purchasers of agricultural products. Both Japan and South Korea, for example, made this transition as recipients of food aid to major markets for American commercial agricultural exports. The Argentinean government was a justifiably frequent complainer to the CSD of the effects of concessional sales on their actual and potential markets and the changes in the rules of the CSD game in the 1960s was a recognition of the adverse affects that concessional sales were having on the international competitive process. However, as has been noted, these changes were more cosmetic than real.

While the original major concerns with the emerging world food aid policy, that is to say American food aid policy, were to safeguard international agricultural trade from dumping and unfair competition. Other donors of food aid were emerging in the late 1950s and 1960s, most notably Canada and Australia (Mettrick, 1969). The value of food as a form of aid was beginning to be questioned, particularly in the United States of America where benefits to recipients of food aid were coming under scrutiny as was the costs of PL 480 to the American taxpayer. Professor Schultz (1960) particularly highlighted the value of this highly tied form of commodity aid to both donor and recipient, suggesting that food aid in value terms was not as beneficial as had been asserted by the food aid administration. In his seminal article Schultz argued that far from being a beneficial form of aid, there was a real danger that food aid would undermine the productive capacity of the recipient country and prove detrimental to the agricultural prospects of the recipient. Food aid would displace home production and thus be detrimental and positively harmful to the recipients. Schultz had pointed out in simple and forceful terms, that the dangers to competition that had concerned the international community, were also present within recipient countries.

Price Displacement or the displacement effects of food aid have been a major concern of all food programmes since the 1960s and the debate about these potential and actual effects have been hotly discussed and disputed for thirty-five years (for a recent discussion of these see Maxwell, 1991). The emerging consensus amongst food aid experts on displacement effects is that they are real, but need not necessarily be harmful if they are monitored and the appropriate policy adjustments made within the agricultural and welfare policy of the recipient country, so as to ensure that the net benefits of the aid are realised. The monitoring and prevention of adverse price displacement effects is still, however, subject to many qualifications and is by no means an insignificant problem.

The PL 480 Programme by the end of the 1950s was beginning to show serious signs of major problems. The programme itself was becoming costly and unwieldy; it had grown rapidly during its early years and many recipient countries had become major dependants on US food aid with an increased likelihood that this dependence would continue. The American farm programmes that were supplying PL 480 were becoming more and more costly and these problem multiplying effects suggested that the farm problem (of increasing productivity) could not be solved by price supports and export subsidy programmes. In addition to the problems of international competition being undermined and the spiralling cost of the US farm programme, the administration of PL 480 in recipient countries was proving very problematic.

Recipients of PL 480 concessional sales, sold these commodities on their internal markets and the resulting revenues known as counterpart funds were deposited, usually in the recipient central bank in the name of the PL 480 administration or of the USAID authorities. The US authorities in recipient countries were required to agree the use of these funds with the recipient government. Counterpart funds accumulated into large deposits with many recipient central banks. These funds, by virtue of their size, were becoming an embarrassment to the American aid authorities since they were not, and could not, be spent. The effects of releasing these vast sums of money in a number of recipient countries were likely to increase the money supply, since they were held by the central bank, and cause inflationary pressures and macro-economic instability within the recipient economy. That these counterpart funds had already been used in the economies concerned and were therefore not real resources, was an argument that gained support, as well as the sheer size of counterpart funds, persuading the American authorities that they were not likely to be spent and therefore it was necessary to write them off and abandon their future accumulation.

The early 1960s saw a major reappraisal of American food aid policy as a result of the growing national cost of this policy and the international misgivings with regard to PL 480. A number of countries in the developing world also had misgivings with regard to the benefits of food aid, most notably India, who began to object to the conditions that the US aid authorities were applying to further and future food donations. As part of the reappraisal of PL 480 the United States changed the view it had held since the establishment of the Food and Agricultural Organisation of the United Nations in the late 1940s, and accepted that there was a limited role for multilateral food aid. The United States was opposed to giving powers, authority and resources to the FAO to oversee world agricultural trade and food policy on the grounds that the policies proposed by the FAO would hamper world agricultural trade and growth.

The FAO from its very inception had its potential role as an organisation to address issues of food and agriculture of a global nature constrained and narrowed, largely because of the objection of the United States (see Boyd-Orr, 1966). Its role in world agriculture was largely confined to data gathering and co-ordination of technical functions and has never had the degree of influence on shaping policies that has been accorded to the International Monetary Fund, the World Bank or the General Agreement on Tariffs and Trade who were established in the same era as the FAO. The policies advocated by the FAO with regard to agricultural production and trade involved intervention in markets, for a variety of objectives including price stabilisation, stockholding policies and general interventions in markets for social and welfare policies and objectives. The FAO was also concerned with the estimation of the extent of hunger and malnutrition in the world. The FAO's role in formulating world policies with regard to hunger and malnutrition was largely thwarted during the 1950s and its inability to establish itself in subsequent decades has made its influence on the shaping of agricultural and food policies in the world economy a pale shadow of what its role was hoped to be when it was established at Hot Springs in 1943 (for a further discussion of the FAO see Talbot, 1990 and Hancock, 1990).

The FAO did sponsor a seminal study, under its Freedom from Hunger Campaign of the 1960s which persuaded the US to accept a UN agency to distribute food aid for development purposes. The report of the Committee, chaired by H.W. Singer, Development through Food (Rome, 1962) proposed amongst other things that food aid could provide valuable resources for social and economic development in developing countries. In reviewing the role of food as aid, Development through Food argued a role for the United Nations as a multilateral provider of food aid as a development resource. The report sought to identify categories of countries that would potentially benefit from surplus food from rich countries and the report also identified a policy framework in which food aid could operate on a multilateral level. The report argued in effect for an alternative policy framework to the predominant American food aid policy that would specialise on project lending funded by food donations from the international community, not just the United States. Although the US was the major contributor of food surpluses to the programme.

The WFP was established with voluntary pledges of food, cash and shipping services. The target which was not reached was $100 million. Three quarters of the Programme resources were food and the remaining balance was made up of cash and services. The US gave 50% of the total with Western Europe contributing 30% (of which EFTA [European Free Trade Area] gave 16% and the EEC 14%). The EEC in its contribution pledge was in fact less generous than EFTA, where Denmark, Sweden and Norway were more enthusiastic supporters of the WFP. The United Kingdom, together with the EFTA members, increased their pledges (see Wightman, 1968). In addition the report identified areas of national economic development where food aid had a role to play such as National Food Reserves (previously proposed by the FAO in 1958).

Development through Food argued the case for a multilateral role in the United Nations for a niche UN provision of food aid. The report was accepted by the UN system and the proposal to establish a multilateral agency, the World Food Programme was agreed (WFP). The WFP came into being in 1963 on a three-year experimental basis which was subsequently renewed. The World Food Programme has maintained a separate multilateral identify and has operated separately from the Food and Agricultural Organisation of the UN, specialising in identifying projects for social and economic development and resisting pressure to focus its entire activities on providing food aid as emergency and relief aid (for a discussion of the food aid policies and programme of the World Food Programme see Shaw and Clay, 1993). The US accepted a role for a multilateral food aid agency as indeed did the European Economic Community who were signatories to the establishment of the World Food Programme, other European countries (such as the United Kingdom) who would be future members of the European Union were also signatories to the establishment of the World Food Programme.

The establishment of the WFP was the first occasion that the European Community as an entity began to formulate a view on food aid as a development resource albeit as part of an international UN focused initiative. Many of the policy concerns of the WFP, and particularly those concerns that involve interventions in the market place such as promoting buffer stock and price stabilisation policies, have also been part of the thinking of European food aid policy. The policy prescriptions of the four Rome Food and Agricultural Agencies, that is to say the Food and Agricultural Organisation (FAO), the World Food Programme (WFP) and the World Food Council (WFC) and the International Fund for Agricultural Development (IFAD) generally favour interventions in agricultural markets, as does the policies of the European Union. European food aid and its policy framework has had a close similarity with that of the Rome food agencies and the policy prescriptions are based upon similar premises with regard to appropriate policies and policy frameworks to promote agricultural development and growth, as well as alleviate hunger and malnutrition.

The emergence of a European Union interest in food aid policy pre-dates the establishment of its own separate food aid programme and that initial support for a multilateral UN Agency the World Food Programme was the beginning of a separate emerging European Union view on food as a source of aid and as a development resource, and was as important a starting point for a European policy as was the establishment of its own self-funded programme. The acceptance of the principles of surplus disposal as a safeguard to competition in international agricultural trade, albeit less than ideal, and the participation in the establishment of the World Food Programme, both provided Europe as an entity, the opportunity to focus on food aid as a potential development resource and in time to develop its own independent programme.

The early 1960s saw the establishment in the European Economic Community of the six of a protectionist Common Agricultural Policy (CAP) with its aims of achieving self-sufficiency in agricultural production by intervention in markets to realise these aims. The economic integration of Europe, while beginning with a Customs Union Policy (CUP) was developed quickly to include a wider policy integration than trade policy itself. The CAP was established for the integration of European agriculture, social and regional policy frameworks were also put in place. The European Community sought to develop common policies in a number of spheres including foreign aid.

The Common Agricultural Policy with its self-sufficiency objectives was designed to exclude foreign food imports in favour of European produced commodities. This policy would result in the emergence of surplus agricultural capacity within Europe and with it the interference in world agricultural trade and the reduction of competition with regard to agricultural production, affecting amongst other countries, the European markets of the United States of America.

1.2 The establishment of the European food aid programme, 1968

The birth of the European food aid policy and separate programme was a direct outcome of the International Wheat Agreement (IWA) of 1967 with its introduction of the first Food Aid Convention (FAC). The IWA was itself part of a desire to promote liberalisation in international agricultural trade, although at this time strictly speaking agriculture was not then an integral part of the General Agreement on Tariffs and Trade (GATT) and therefore the achievements of tariff reductions during the Kennedy Round fell mainly on the manufacturing trade sector (see Bhagwati, 1988). During the period of the 1940s and 1950s American agriculture, as previously discussed, expanded its export markets with a combination of concessional sales (food aid) and commercial sales. In the 1930s the US had an average of 15% of world trade in grains, but by the 1960s this had grown to some 40% of the world grain trade. The rate of growth of US agricultural trade, however, was slowing and the costs of concessional sales was becoming a burden on the US taxpayer as well as becoming a self-defeating programme (see Cathie, 1985 for further discussion). The emergence of a European Common Agricultural Policy also signalled to the US that both an agricultural policy reform as well as a (food aid) concessional sales policy reform was required as a matter of urgency.

The world grains market of the 1950s provided the United States with opportunities for increasing its market share and it was not in the immediate interests of this expansion to embrace agriculture within the liberalisation rules of the GATT. By the 1960s, however, the world market situation was beginning to change and with it the need for a change in US policy. It was not until the Uruguay Round of the GATT in the 1990s that agricultural trade was more fully incorporated into that

17

agreement as part of the negotiations and of the final agreement. The United States as well as other agricultural trading countries (the Cairns Group[1]) pressed the Europeans and the Japanese to liberalise their agricultural trade practice by reducing their levels of agricultural protection.

The International Wheat Agreement had originally been established in the interwar period as a response to the instability of commodity prices and the collapse of international markets that characterised the commodity price collapse of the 1920s and the Great Depression of the 1930s. Commodity agreements at that time were considered as a means of dealing with the disequilibrium between supply and demand on international markets. Agreements were concluded in the 1920s for rubber, sugar, tin and tea. The agreements aimed, by forming cartels, to reconcile the interests of producers and consumers by attempting to stabilise prices or output. In practice these arrangements did not achieve their objectives. The problems of stabilising commodity markets were investigated by the League of Nations with a view to establishing whether these agreements had achieved their objectives, particularly the Wheat Agreement of 1933 and the Sugar Agreement of 1937. The agreements had in fact not been successful (see van Meerhaeghe, 1971).

After the Second World War, in 1947, a new Convention was adopted and the International Wheat Council was established in London. In 1949 a Wheat agreement was signed by forty-seven countries with the general objective of assuring supplies of wheat to importing and exporting countries at equitable and stable prices. The agreement lasted four years until 1953; extensions of three years were made during the years 1956, 1959, 1962 and 1967. Cereals discussions were attempted in the Kennedy Round of GATT negotiations in 1963, and in 1967 the basic elements of the grains arrangement were re-negotiated. The International Grains Arrangement of 1967 adopted two legal instruments: the Wheat Trade Convention and the Food Aid Convention.

The United States, during the 1950s, as virtually the sole supplier of surplus agricultural commodities, had also resumed the whole burden of the international supply management of the grain market. In addition to the PL 480 concessional sales programme, the US also carried large and accumulating carry-over grain stocks with increasing taxpayer costs. The United States signalled during the Kennedy Round of the GATT that they were no longer prepared to assume the burden of international supply management, or the increasing cost of a de facto world food aid provision.

In the establishment of the WFP there had been an attempt by the US, in the pledging formulae adopted, to address the burden-sharing issue of food aid, but as has been seen, the EEC particularly were unwilling to assume a larger share of the cost of the WFP than they had agreed at 14% of the total costs. The EEC, Britain and Japan, were reluctant to have food aid as part of the International Grains Agreement of 1967, but given that the quid pro quo for accepting the FAC was the prospects of stabilisation of the world grain market, they agreed. Without the International Grains Agreement and the FAC, the United States was not prepared to offer further concessions in the Kennedy Round on industrial products (see Wightman, 1968).

The United States had initially proposed a minimum contribution of 10 million tonnes to the Food Aid Convention. However, negotiations reduced this minimum to 4.5 million tonnes. The European Community agreed to provide 23% of the contribution to the Convention. The Convention also established a Food Aid Committee of all the donors to monitor and record food aid shipments. The emphasis in the FAC was that the giving of food aid multilaterally was desirable, although it was recognised that most of the food aid that would be given under this Convention would, in fact, be bilateral. The FAC of 1967 was renewed in 1971 with the new International Wheat Agreement of that year. Although given the world wheat market conditions of rising prices, the minimum annual contribution fell to less than 4 million tonnes. The FAC was extended in 1980 to 1986 when the minimum contribution was raised to 7.6 million tonnes (although the World Food Conference of the 1970s had proposed a minimum of at least 10 million tonnes as a target for food aid under the FAC). At the beginning of the 1970s when world market conditions had changed from surplus to shortage and stocks had been depleted and prices of grains had risen to unprecedented levels, the FAC did provide the basic minimum annual flow of 4 million tons. Food aid, in fact, in the early 1970s, exceeded 12.5 million tons, the 8 million tonnes being largely provided by the United States in the form of concessional sales, or on credit at low interest rates (see Parotte, 1983).

The FAC of the International Wheat Agreement was designed primarily as a means of spreading the responsibility of the costs of international food aid; it did not increase the total supply of food aid, but re-distributed its costs amongst agricultural exporting and importing countries. The FAC was a means of establishing a greater collective responsibility for the provision and financing of food aid, in so far as both exporters and importers were to be involved in sharing the costs of food aid which had hitherto been the sole responsibility of the exporters. The EEC, and particularly France, were reluctant to accept any form of collective action on the provision of food aid and European contributions to its FAC commitments in the late 1960s, were to be predominantly multilateral and channelled through the World Food Programme.

On July 1st 1968 the European Economic Community joined the FAC of the International Wheat Agreement, and a European food aid programme had been established with some reluctance on behalf of the Community, but in recognition of the American insistence on the sharing of the burden of the supply management and cost of the international grains market. The EEC had thus accepted that it would contribute more directly, and with a larger share of the cost, to the supply of world food aid, than it had been prepared to do under its commitment to the WFP in 1963.

European food aid policy emerged as a consequence of the relationship between agricultural trade policy in the wheat sector and surplus disposal policies arising from government attempts at supply management of markets at the national and international levels. The surplus disposal experience of the 1940s, 1950s and 1960s had largely been an American experience, however with effects of growing agricultural protection in the Community, structural surpluses began to appear as a consequence of the Common Agricultural Policy. The EEC's own food aid programme did not quite replicate the earlier US experience as a policy purely for surplus disposal. No sooner had the International Wheat Agreement been signed than the world market conditions for grain changed from that of surplus overhang, which characterised the 1950s and 1960s, and a downward pressure on prices, to that of relative scarcity of supplies and stocks to sharply rising prices, particularly after 1972.

The relationship between the supply of food aid and commercial agricultural markets, both at the national, regional and international levels, has played a central part in the design of food aid programmes and

20

in the emphasis that has been given in international agreements to prevent food aid becoming a euphemism for export dumping, or as a source of price displacement in the agricultural sectors of recipient countries. The experience of the US with its own PL 480 programme and the costs of that programme to American taxpayers, and the limits of supply management saw a major change of policy. PL 480 became much more concerned with commercial markets for American farm produce, in so far as the terms of US food aid hardened and the era of surplus disposal ended in the 1970s price rises on the world market. The United States, in anticipating surplus capacity in European agriculture markets because of the CAP, ensured that the EEC would not remain at the margins of world food aid policy but would assume a greater responsibility for the burdens and costs of food aid, than hitherto the Community was prepared to undertake. In its initial conception the EEC food aid programme was largely, although not exclusively, a result of the International Wheat Agreement and the American desire to transfer some of the burden and the responsibility of providing food aid to other countries and particularly to the agriculturally protectionist European Community.

Note

[1] The Cairns Group, formed in 1986/87 to present a common policy on the liberalisation of agricultural trade in the GATT negotiations, were Argentina, Australia, Brazil, Canada, Chile, Colombia, Fiji, Hungary, Indonesia, Malaysia, New Zealand, the Philippines, Thailand and Uruguay.

2 The development of a European food aid policy since 1968

2.1   The food aid convention and its development

When Europe became a signatory to the International Wheat Agreement of 1967 with its Food Aid Convention, it had undertaken an international commitment to increase its support for food aid donations to developing countries. The Community had made an earlier commitment in support of food aid, as a development instrument, when it contributed to the establishment of the UN multilateral agency, the World Food Programme in 1963. While it did not establish its own Community programme until 1968, it had accepted a role for food aid as a development instrument.

The International Wheat Agreement at the behest of the US, was itself more concerned with world market price stability and with competition and the potential threat to competition from the emerging protectionist agricultural policies of the EEC. The Food Aid Convention was established as an adjunct to the primary purpose of the wheat agreement and its objectives, rather than as a means of increasing the total supply of world food aid. The FAC did in fact cause the European Community to increase its food aid commitment from what it had previously been prepared to undertake with its support of the World Food Programme. The Americans had proposed an FAC target of 10 million tonnes but the Europeans preferred the lower target of some 4.5 million tonnes since they had not wished to include the FAC in the wheat agreement. The burden-sharing of food aid costs amongst cereal importers and cereal exporters was as much the purpose of the Convention as it was the increase of the total supply of cereals as food aid. The proposal for the FAC was American and it was based upon both the rising costs of its own food aid programme and the clear linking of its PL 480 concessional sales programme to the commercial market development of the world cereals market.

As part of the IWA and the wider Kennedy Round trade negotiations of the GATT, Europe increased its food aid commitment and established its own programme. European support for multilateral food aid had been given to the World Food Programme since 1963, without the need for a separate Community managed own food aid programme. The Agricultural Directorate (DG VI) (see Chapter Four for Directorates concerned with food aid policy p.80) and its procurement agencies provided the European commitment to the WFP. Since the aid committed at that time was relatively modest there was no need to establish a separate procurement agency from that available within the Agricultural Directorate.

The European food aid programme was concerned initially with one food commodity, cereals, and in 1968 the six donated 1 million tonnes as aid. By 1970 the Union had added other commodities to its programme, most notably skimmed milk powder was added to the commodities available for aid and donated through the World Food Programme. PL 480 had, throughout the 1950s and 1960s, provided a wide variety of agricultural products in its concessional sales programme, including raw cotton and tobacco (see Cathie, 1989). PL 480, in its wide agricultural commodity coverage, was a programme that was designed to aid the agricultural sector of the economy as a whole, by raising general output. The range of commodities of both food and fibre attests to this broad purpose. The European programme throughout its twenty-five years of operations has not, in the range of commodities it has made available as aid, ever reached the range of agricultural commodities that the PL 480 programme offered. PL 480 was a general surplus disposal programme for American agricultural interests and producers, where concessional and commercial market opportunities were being developed in recipient economies and the presumption of the PL 480 was that the interests of all agricultural producers in the US would be served under this aid programme.

Thus American food aid policy was a broad policy embracing the whole agricultural sector whereas the European programme has been selective in the commodities available as aid and not all surplus agricultural commodities within the Community have been available as aid. Wine has been in surplus within the community and has been removed from the market by denaturing rather than being offered under its aid programme. Other commodities that have not proved suitable as aid have been removed from the market by distruction or storage. Perishable vegetables are destroyed thus removing them from the market. Beef is removed from the market into cold storage and is occasionally given under the food aid programme, although this form of food as aid has caused problems with high transport costs and distribution problems due to refrigeration and storage requirements.

The Union donations of beef to Russia and West Africa in the 1990s both proved to be unsatisfactory, attracting criticism in the media. The EEC food aid programme was never overtly a surplus agricultural disposal programme whereas the US programme saw a 'marriage of convenience' between the interests of US agricultural producers and agricultural commodities as a source of foreign aid assistance as well as the development of markets within recipient countries. The European Community has never argued the case for food as a form of aid on the grounds of the interests of its own producers and future community markets and community market development. The surplus disposal element in food aid programmes, especially drawing from the PL 480 experience and practice of the 1950s and 1960s, lay behind the inclusion of the FAC in the International Wheat Agreement and the concern that food aid could be a means of unfair competition and market development. The European Community has not considered food as aid on the grounds of surplus disposal but on the grounds of competition within the world cereals market and as a development resource having value for the recipient.

The International Wheat Agreement of 1967 was agreed under conditions in the world market that were to rapidly change, the overhang of cereals stocks were to reduce and, taken together with the change in US agricultural policy and food aid policy, the surplus era was to end as cereal prices on world market began to climb. The intention of the IWA of 1967 was to provide a floor on cereal prices, but in the event by 1974 world wheat prices reached levels that had not been seen in the post war period (including the Korean war period of the early 1950s). The instability on world food markets had not resulted from the downward pressure on price, but from the rapid rise in prices of cereals and other agricultural commodities as well as primary commodities in general.

One lasting legacy of the IWA of 1967 and the subsequent agreements has been the Food Aid Convention. The IWAs of 1967, 1971 and 1980 have not achieved their market stability objectives, however the FACs have been renewed and the minimum contributions of the signatories to the Conventions have been from 4,259 tonnes in 1967, dropping to 3,974 in 1971, and increasing to 7,612 in 1980. During the 1980s cereals food aid has exceeded the minimum FAC of 7,517 tonnes and has averaged near to the 10 million tonnes originally proposed in the first 1967 Convention. The Food Aid Convention as part of the IWA's attempts to ensure stability in the international wheat market has played a minimum if not irrelevant role, since the wheat agreements of the period have been overtaken by market events. The FACs have provided an opportunity for some agreement on the signatories' commitment to total cereals food aid as a minimum commitment.

The relevance of the FACs for the international cereals market must remain in some doubt, since the main purposes of the IWAs have not been realised when market conditions changed as they did in the 1970s. World food aid donations are a residual to the ineffective IWAs, and when an agreement could not be made in 1980 the link was severed between the IWA and the FAC. The FAC of 1980 attempted to include food commodities other than cereals, however the historic link with the wheat agreements is still maintained, although the surplus era of the 1960s which had brought about the Food Aid Convention had long since passed. The cereals food aid requirement of the developing world is not based upon the effective need for cereals as aid but loosely upon the targets of past conventions. From time to time estimates are made on the basis of potential demand for cereals aid (e.g. Huddleston, 1981).

However, the FAC is not a food aid donor agency but is an agreement amongst exporters and importers for a minimum commitment of cereals as aid. FAC minimum targets have become a reference point in the food aid community on world targets, but beyond that its relevance to cereals aid and the potential trade and surplus disposal effects have largely become overtaken by events. World food aid policy has spawned institutions and conventions, such as the Committee on Surplus Disposals and the Food Aid Convention which have played a minimum role, and were designed to do, in monitoring food aid either as a disruption to trade, or markets. Europe was not enthusiastic about the cereals FAC from its inception and has sought to widen its role to include other food aid commodities (namely dairy products). The Community has increased its minimum contributions as it has enlarged from 1,035 tonnes in 1967 to 1,650 tonnes in 1980 and 1,670 tonnes in 1987. The UK was a signatory to the 1967 FAC Convention but did not sign the 1971 Convention, although on its accession to the Community rejoined in 1973. The accession of Austria, Sweden and Finland to the EU who were signatories of the FAC in 1987, will increase the Union share of world food aid by some 3%, to 25% of the total.

2.2   The evolution of the cereals food aid programme

The European Community of the six allocated its Community food aid actions as opposed to the national food aid programmes largely through the WFP multilateral agency, procuring the necessary cereals and cash to meet its FAC commitments. During the first FAC (1967-71) National actions and Community actions taken together met the minimum target requirements. The Community food aid programme was largely the fulfilment of the FAC through the WFP, rather than the development of its own particular food aid policies and programmes.

European food aid policy was, in its early years, a mixture of both multilateral policy and the bilateral policies of France, Germany, Italy, the Netherlands and Belgium and Luxembourg. Belgium and Luxembourg are considered to have one joint programme. Europe had in effect six food aid programmes and European policy could be portrayed as either bilateral or multilateral. The EEC, Community food aid actions, because they were given to the WFP or the Red Cross for distribution, were generally referred to by the Commission as multilateral. From 1968 to 1972 EEC food aid policy as Community actions was in support of the multilateral food aid policies of the WFP and the emerging programmes of the private NGOs (non-governmental organisations) and that of the Red Cross Societies. Since the WFP favoured the project approach to the use of food aid and the Red Cross was involved with food as a means of providing relief and rehabilitation, neither agencies were liable to cause the trade dumping problems that the FAC had been designed to monitor.

The FAC of 1971 re-confirmed the EEC earlier commitment, and the total Convention commitment had fallen largely because the UK and Denmark did not join the Convention of 1971. They did become members along with Ireland in 1973 when the three countries joined the Community. By 1973 the European commitment under the 1971 FAC raised the European FAC commitment from 1,035 (000) tonnes, to 1,161 (000) tonnes.

During the period 1972-74 world food aid fell from the established levels of the 1950s and 1960s where 14,000 million tonnes were not uncommon as an annual food aid commitment over these decades (Wallerstein, 1980). In the mid-1960s 18,000 million tonnes were a frequent annual PL 480 food aid volumes.

Fig.1 shows that between 1971 and 1974 the volume of world food aid fell to the lowest level it has attained since the inception of food as aid from the Marshall Plan period until the present. During this period 1971 to 1974 as the 'World Food Crisis' emerged, the EEC became the second largest donor to the United States with 20% of total world food aid in 1973/74. As world wheat prices rose so world food aid volume shrank, as did carry-over stocks, and the fundamental conditions of the world wheat market had changed (see next Chapter for further discussion of these issues).

The use of surplus wheat as food aid had gone from surplus to scarcity, as the second Food Aid Convention had not run its course and with it the need for surveillance, of surplus disposals of wheat. European food aid, as is illustrated in Fig.I, has increased over the period 1971-1990 although the years 1974-75 saw a considerable drop to 3.5% of total world food aid. The EEC, with the exception of the years 1974-75, has remained the second major food aid donor in cereals, to that of the United States premier position.

Table I1 shows in greater detail the evolution of the European position with regard to the supply of world food aid. Having provided 20% of world cereals aid in 1973 The Community did not reach this proportion again for a further ten years and in the 1990s its share of world food has begun to rise to a larger proportion, namely 25% of world food aid. As has previously been mentioned, the enlargement of the Union to include

million tonnes

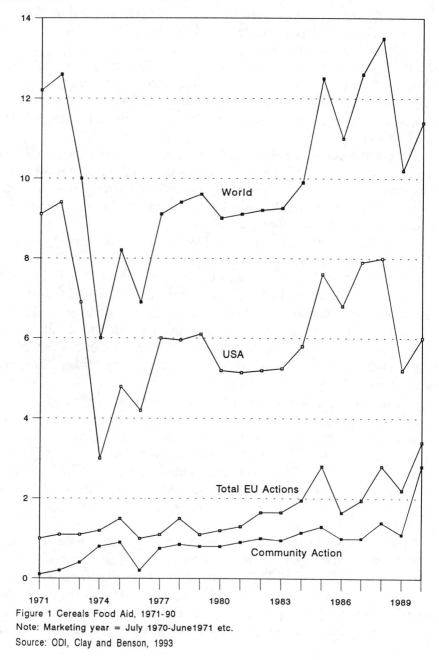

Figure 1 Cereals Food Aid, 1971-90
Note: Marketing year = July 1970-June1971 etc.
Source: ODI, Clay and Benson, 1993

28

Table I

European food aid and national member states food aid (cereals) 1971-90

(thousand tonnes)

	71/72	72/73	73/74	74/75	75/76	76/77	77/78	78/79	79/80	80/81	81/82	82/83	83/84	84/85	85/86	86/87	88/90
Belgium & Luxembourg	31.0	41.7	45.8	35.5	42.8	48.0	53.8	41.0	52.3	27.9	34.4	31.7	29.9	96.7	29.1	30.5	35.0
Denmark	-	-	6.2	25.8	14.2	16.5	54.5	30.8	7.8	7.8	33.2	17.2	18.5	25.0	-	24.9	47.0
France	142.7	209.6	197.5	113.0	180.5	135.5	188.5	126.3	167.3	143.8	197.8	202.4	297.0	262.5	87.6	256.3	226.0
Germany	261.7	206.1	226.0	140.0	159.0	165.2	149.6	140.7	141.5	178.6	197.4	172.0	160.6	347.4	196.0	183.9	302.0
Greece													8.0	9.0	14.2	7.5	6.0
Ireland	-	-	10.3	74.7	5.6	3.0	4.2	3.7	4.8	4.0	4.4	9.6	4.1	6.0	1.3	4.7	3.0
Italy	95.0	36.0	63.1	27.6	67.8	57.4	37.9	29.9	99.4	51.7	104.7	120.7	55.2	173.7	125.3	112.3	195.0
Netherlands	58.6	58.9			54.2	87.3	111.2	94.2	34.9	92.6	77.9	50.5	138.1	150.9	120.2	113.9	156.0
Spain										14.0	22.3	25.5	26.5	36.1	27.8	23.5	40.0
United Kingdom	193.7	113.3	56.2	125.3	106.8	65.0	65.1	80.6	100.6	57.2	83.1	125.1	154.4	137.6	95.7	153.3	144.0
Total National Actions	782.7	665.6	604.3	541.9	630.9	575.9	664.8	547.2	608.6	577.6	755.2	754.7	892.3	1244.9	697.2	910.8	1152.0
EEC Food Aid (Community Actions)	195.7	320.5	604.2	871.2	297.0	555.2	709.1	611.7	597.0	714.0	846.6	840.8	1024.4	1259.2	916.9	946.8	1765.0
Total National Actions + EC Community Actions	978.4	986.1	1208.6	1413.1	927.9	1131.1	1375.9	1158.9	1205.6	1291.6	1601.8	1596.4	1916.7	2504.1	1614.1	1857.6	2916.0
Total World Food Aid (Cereals)	1251.8	9964.1	5818.7	8399.4	6847.0	9022.4	9215.5	9499.7	8887.0	8942.2	9140.2	9198.0	9831.0	12462.6	10949.2	12403.6	12946.0
EC Food Aid and National Actions as percentage of total world food aid	7.8	9.8	20.7	16.8	3.5	12.5	14.9	12.1	13.5	14.4	17.5	17.3	19.4	16.4	14.7	14.9	22.5

Source: *Food Aid in Figures*, FAO, various issues.

Austria, Sweden and Finland will increase its share further. It is also likely that future enlargements would increase the agricultural capacity of the Union and possibly its share of cereals food aid as a proportion of world food aid.

Community food aid projected its multilateral character essentially because of its donations to the WFP, and from 1968 until 1974 it would be accurate to say that EEC food aid policy was set by the programmes and policies of World Food Programme. National actions, and national food aid programmes far outweighed Community programmes in volume terms until the balance changed in the mid-1970s in the aftermath of the 'world's food crisis'. From the mid-1970s Community actions became proportionately to exceed the combined national food aid programmes of the enlarged European Union, in volume terms. National food aid programmes, as shown in Table I, account for a substantial share of at least a half, of European food aid donations. Policy has developed gradually over the period where Community actions have come to exceed combined national actions. The EU has gradually moved away from characterising its Community actions as multilateral since its own actions are much nearer to that of a single European action, akin to a national or bilateral programme. The national food aid programmes, of which there are now fourteen, taken together with the EU Programme, contain a wide diversity of views on the effectiveness of food aid as a development resource. The Nation states differ considerably on their views of the role of food aid as a resource for development and not surprisingly the Community's own programme reflects aspects of these national programmes as well as other influences which will be discussed further and in Chapters Four and Five.

While EU or Community actions have increased proportionately over the period since 1974, national food aid policies still are a substantial share of total European food aid. National programmes in volume terms (as indicated by Table I) has Germany as the largest national programme, followed by France, Italy, the Netherlands, the United Kingdom, Belgium and Luxembourg, Denmark, Spain, Ireland and Greece. To some degree the volume of cereals aid given over the period reflects the individual European nation's own view of the role of food as aid. Market conditions have determined the supply of cereals as has the changing requirements with regard to emergency and relief operations, particularly associated

30

with the world food crisis of the 1970s and the African food crisis of the mid-1980s. Both these events have added impetus to the increase in food aid volumes from both the EU programme and the national programmes.

With the singular exception of the United Kingdom, and with due allowance for the annual variability of the national programmes, the trend to increase the volume of Community food aid is clear, giving the EU programme both a larger share of world food aid and the larger share of overall European food aid. The figures indicate the slow but sure emergence of an overall Community programme and actions in cereals food aid. The national food aid programmes, subject to some years of variability, have also increased in volume terms. By the 1990s, with the exception of the United Kingdom, all national food aid programmes have increased the volumes of aid given at the end of the period as compared with the initial donations in the earlier periods as is indicated in Table I.

Table II
EU community actions and national states actions:
total food aid expenditure in 1991

	ECU (million)	% of Total EU
Member States' Actions of which:	384.9	37.6
Denmark	31.0	3.0
France	32.4	3.2
Germany	111.7	10.9
Greece	1.6	0.2
Italy	48.6	4.8
Netherlands	48.5	4.7
UK	60.0	5.9
Others	51.1[a]	5.0
Community Action	637.9	62.4
Total EU[b]	1022.8	100.0

Source: European Commission and Member States.

Notes: a. Total expenditure of Belgium, Ireland, Luxembourg, Portugal and Spain assumed as 5% of total EU aid.
b. Provisional estimate including assumed expenditure of five Member States (see note a).

ODI. Evaluation of EU Food Aid Programme 1994.

31

The position of the EU Community actions in relation the national state's food aid programmes in expenditure terms for 1991 indicates that the Community expenditure is some 62.4% of the total food aid budget for that year and the national programmes the remaining 39% (see Table II). EU Community Policy has become the largest overall component of European food aid programmes both in volume terms and in terms of the total food aid budget of the Union.

2.3 The community food aid programme and the national food aid programmes

While the EU Community food aid programme has, over the last twenty-seven years, become the largest European programme in volume and value terms, the National programmes taken together still remain as significant contributors to the European food aid contribution to world supplies. The EU as a Community as well as the member states, as nation states have not as yet converged their food aid policies into one unified European food aid policy, but rather it is made up of some fifteen Programmes (fourteen National Programmes and the EU Programme).

The Union, particularly with the Single European Act and the Maastricht Agreement seeks to harmonise and unify its economic policies, including a single currency, as well as forming a common foreign and defence policy in a political union. As is well known, the original customs union was designed to promote ever closer union leading to the harmonisation of economic policies and leading to political union (see Johnson, 1965 for an early view). This policy movement has gathered pace since the Treaty of Rome and subsequent enlargements such as the Single European Act, as well as the Maastricht Agreement. The major policy changes in the European framework have sought to move beyond harmonisation to full integration of economic and political matters within the union and with regard to a common policy to the rest of the world. The principle of subsidiarity has been elaborate as a means of allying fears of centralised political authority over the development of common European Union policies. Subsidiarity as a principle is to allow the nation state, the region, or the locality within the Union-responsibility for policy appropriate to those levels, however subsidiarity is unlikely to provide a

32

means for alternative policies to those agreed at the level of overall union policy. Food aid policy as a subset of Union aid and trade policies towards the developing world is part of a policy set that has been evident in the European Community from its origins in the Treaty of Rome in the 1950s (see Chapter Four for a further discussion).

As yet the European Union food aid policy runs parallel to fourteen national food aid policies, while it is possible to refer to a common European policy with regard to food aid, it is equally possible to refer to some fifteen different European policies with food as aid. Europe does not have a common food aid policy but a mixture of policy emphasis which reflects the different views held within Europe by the national states, on the usefulness of food as aid to developing countries. European food aid policy does, through its acceptance of the FAC, the principles of surplus disposal and the contributions to the WFP, have the elements of a common policy that has in fact been determined by extra-European factors, namely the fears, particularly those of the US, of surplus disposal becoming the dominant factor in the emergent European programme. The EU food aid programme has adhered to the surplus disposal fears of the 1950s and 1960s in so far as the policy promoted in the Union has not sought to emulate the policy emphasis of the PL 480 programme of the 1950s and 1960s, whereby the commercial farm interest, the trade interest, and the aid interest were firmly in accord with overall foreign policy objectives (see next Chapter for a further discussion of the surplus disposal issue).

The European food aid policy of the Union has the elements of an *acquis communitaire*, but since it also co-exists with the national programmes, its distinctiveness is always subject to national food aid programme changes both in terms of the volumes of aid being made available to the Community programme, or to the national programmes. The nation states can increase or decrease their contributions to the community programme, as they can increase or decrease their own programmes, as they consider appropriate to their own national objectives. The annual variability in volumes of the national food aid programmes (see Table I) suggests that contributions to the Community programme are decided in the context of the overall food aid contribution of the national states. The European Unions food aid policy is still dependant upon its role as a co-ordinator of the overall food aid policy of the nation states and its own union programme. Since the mid-1980s both the Council of Ministers and the European Parliament have pressed for clear co-ordination of Community and national food aid programmes, arguing for the effective harmonisation of overall policy with regard to European food aid supplies and policy.

The Development Assistance Committee (DAC) of the OECD recorded EU and other donors' expenditure on food aid during the 1980s, however since 1989 in its DAC annual reports it no longer includes food aid expenditure. Community Actions during the late 1980s saw food aid averaging 15% of its Overseas Development Assistance, the national food programmes were in the same period averaging some 5% of their respective aid programmes, including their contributions to Union and multilateral programmes (OECD, 1989). The European Union and the national food aid programmes,while having a common commitment to international obligations such as the principles of surplus disposal and the Food Aid Convention also have subtle differences of emphasis in their respective views of food as an effective form of development assistance.

Community policy emerges in a complex, if not complicated fashion and will be discussed in Chapter Four. While the organisation of national food aid policies of the members of the EU varies considerably from each other and the policy emphasis of a number of programmes have changed over time. Member states, in making a contribution to the WFP and becoming signatories to the FAC in the 1960s, in effect opted to support food aid in the multilateral context as a resource for development assistance. In the main, this support took the form of food and financial resources to the WFP for either small project-based food aid programmes in many developing countries and in support of emergency food supplies for relief and rehabilitation projects (see Cathie, 1982). The resources given to the WFP and resources given to the Red Cross were in the form of outright grants or gifts. Member states of the Union, most notably the Netherlands, Ireland, Denmark, Sweden and Italy have been very supportive of WFP policy on the use of food in project focused development assistance programmes and in their own national food aid programmes have strongly emphasised multilateral policies as the appropriate means to use food aid effectively in development projects. For other members of the Union their national food aid programme reflects their commitment to their share of the FAC agreement; Belgium,

Luxembourg, Ireland, Greece being particular examples of this FAC obligation.

National food aid programmes differ in the way in which food aid policy is formulated in the Netherlands, Italy, Ireland, Denmark, Germany and the United Kingdom. Food aid is part of development policy and is organised by their respective development co-operation ministries as part of overall aid policy. Although within national development agencies as in the United Kingdom and Italy, there are separate units responsible for food aid policy. In France, Germany and Italy, Ministries of Agriculture or intervention boards, are involved in the procurement of supplies and have a consultative role in food aid policy issues. Since both France, Italy and Germany are large overall contributors to European food aid supplies , this direct link to agricultural agencies suggests that the surplus disposal aspect of food aid is still reflected in the procurement of supplies. France and Germany involve a number of agencies in the determination of their respective food aid policies, and this has resulted in a wide variety of influences upon programmes and policies. France, through an inter-agency co-ordinating Committee involves considerations of foreign trade, transport and shipping, while Germany has a national agency for technical co-operation with the capacity to organise food aid projects within its technical co-operation programmes.

The different ways in which food aid and, indeed, development policies are organised within the member states of the European Union, indicate to some degree the origins of the form of development assistance as a secondary outcome of issues relating to surplus disposal competition and agricultural trade. These historic features of the national food aid programmes and policies, do not equally apply to the fourteen national states since very different views of the role of food in the development of recipient countries is a feature of all the national states. The nation states hold a variety of views on issues relating to food and agricultural policy within the Union, and particularly the role of agriculture and appropriate targets and instruments of policy.

The spectrum ranges from that of the UK's emphasis on free trade in agricultural products with its objective of low cost food supplies for consumers, to that of self-sufficiency of agricultural production, as with France, and the higher prices for consumers that this entails. The

Common Agricultural Policy (CAP), in addition to that of being a policy on the food supply, is a policy on the social and regional dimensions of agriculture, and this is reflected in the variety and range of policies, institutions and priorities that are to be seen in the member states' own food and agricultural policies and programmes. The CAP is a compromise that has not entirely changed national views on agricultural policy with regard to its social and economic roles. Since its origins in the 1960s the CAP has been subject to moderation and adaptations, however the fundamental emphasis on both the social and economic objectives of agricultural policy have been adhered to, although the issues of budgetary cost, international trade and the enlargement of the Union have caused periodic crises within the Community.

The different national views of food and agriculture is also reflected in different views on development assistance and in particular the role of food as aid. The national food aid programmes and policies of the members of the Union differ widely on whether food is an appropriate form of development assistance, with the United Kingdom being the most sceptical member state, and the least consistent over time. These differences between the nation states is seen in preferences for small scale project-supported food aid programmes, including food-for-work projects, to large scale programmes with macroeconomic and commercial implications for recipients. Food aid is seen as a means of emergency, relief, rehabilitation and humanitarian assistance, rather than as a development resource equivalent to untied financial aid. Different views are held on the potential for the price displacement effects of food aid, although not on the need to ensure that these potential effects are monitored in programmes and projects. The portmanteau approach of the Union Policy towards food aid and food security policy towards developing countries tends to underplay, not surprisingly, the quite distinctive but subtle differences in food aid priorities that there are between the fourteen national food aid policies.

In addition to the origins of the national food aid programmes and policies, and the national aid and development programmes as well as differing views on agriculture and trade, the nation states have a fundamentally different historic and cultural approach towards government and policy. These historic differences are reflected in national attitudes and policies towards organisation, including aid in general and food aid in particular. The member states can be divided into three groupings: Anglo-Saxon, Latin and Germanic, with preferences for organisation being largely determined in the fifteen member States by these three categories.

The Anglo-Saxons and the Scandinavians have a preference for horizontal structures and for implicit rules with regard to organisation. Small organisations are also preferred. The Latins prefer vertical organisational structures, often monolithic, with clear rules. The Germans are in between the Anglo-Saxons and the Latins, but have a strong preference for rules and regulations. The Anglo-Saxons and the Scandinavians prefer implicit rules, such as those involved with free markets. These differences can be identified from the period of the reformation, and even before this, and have a considerable bearing upon the nation states' views on social and economic policies. The fundamental differences in national and cultural outlook are present in the organisation and policy with regard to aid and food aid, as well as, of course, to wider economic, social and political life in general.

These differences are accommodated in the portmanteau approach of Union Policy, where different strands of national approaches are blended into a bland although not inconsistent overall policy. Rules, regulations and organisational complication and complexity is a characteristic of all Union policies, including food aid policies and programmes. Elements of individual national policies may find a place within overall union policy, however the outcome of this process is Union policy which appears to favour vertical integration with rules, regulations, resolutions and guidelines. Food aid policy at the level of the union is no exception to these tendencies, as will be discussed in Chapter Four where the evolution of Union food aid policies will be given consideration.

German food aid policy

The national food aid policy of Germany, the largest of European donors, emphasises the use of food as a means of providing food security in developing countries. Germany has pioneered triangular transactions, that is the provision of cash to developing countries to purchase food from other developing countries, from the original 1967 FAC. Triangular transactions encourage trade in foodstuffs between developing countries;

in 1991 one third of German cereals aid was covered by these trade related transactions. German food aid policy stresses the importance of developing countries being self-reliant with regard to their food security policies, rather than aiming for self-sufficiency in food production. The food aid programme considers food as a fully costed resource which competes with other aid programmes and projects.

Programme food aid, where its purpose is to provide budgetary support for the recipient, is being discontinued. The purchase of food in Europe, or within developing countries, with the purpose of general budgetary support through the sales of these commodities, is not regarded as an effective means of providing development finance. German food aid policy seeks to improve the overall food situation in developing countries by strengthening the food system in recipient countries. Food aid is therefore now part of a wider food security approach to developing countries, with the twin objectives of the establishment of food security stocks, as part of the recipient government's management of its food system. The second objective is to integrate the use of food aid into wider rural development projects, including food-for-work programmes. These projects either provide food directly or, if the food is sold, that is to say monetised, the ensuing funds are used on a specific pre-planned project.

Programme food aid is now regarded as an infrequent occurrence in German food aid policy. The support for security stocks and food-for-work projects are both features of the multilateral food and agricultural agencies of the FAO and WFP which the Germans have adopted, albeit under a food security priority within its development assistance. German food aid has also responded to the growing need for food for disasters and emergency aid, and for long-term relief to refugees; in 1991 41% of bilateral food aid was allocated for emergency and relief purposes. German food aid policy has broken the link with surplus disposal of agricultural commodities, but recognises a role for food in promoting self-reliance and trade in developing countries. Food aid is part of a wider food security policy set, where it is but one input to promote development. The share of German food aid is also being directed increasingly towards humanitarian objectives, in addition to specific rural development projects and to vulnerable group support.

French food aid policy

The national food aid policy of France, like the German food aid programme, has the twin objectives of humanitarian and development support. However, there is also a more explicit political and commercial purpose underpinning this aid. While the Germans have explicitly broken the link with food aid and surplus disposal, this is not necessarily the case with French policy. France supports recipients with food aid as balance of payments support, where there are structural deficits. As with its own agricultural policy, France supports the objective of self-sufficiency in the recipient country's agricultural policy. This differs from the German emphasis on self-reliance, which implies the purchase of food on world markets, or regional markets as part of a wide food security objective, if this is appropriate to do so.

The sales of French food aid within recipient countries which generates counterpart funds, are earmarked for either rural development projects or for food security stocks. France has not been involved in triangular transactions or local purchases of food since the cereals involved in its food aid programme are bought within France itself. The purchase of food for its aid programme is strongly related to its own agricultural production and its prospects for creating markets in developing countries, and in this sense France, of all the European national food aid programmes, is nearer to the objectives of PL 480 in the 1950s and 1960s. France supports the stock policy objectives of the WFP and the FAO, providing 10% of its national aid to the WFP's International Emergency Food Reserve.

The major country recipient of French cereals aid is Egypt, where approximately one quarter of its food aid is given annually. In line with French foreign policy, food aid is given to Francophone countries, particularly within Africa. Food aid is very much a part of general aid and foreign policy,with the exception of its multilateral contributions and donations are given on a government-to-government basis. Food aid donations as a state activity with commercial and political objectives is the major feature of French policy with non-government organisations exceptionally being given support. This support to NGOs is usually given in countries where French policy and political contact has become imperative such as in Rwanda. Like the German food aid programme, the

French are also increasing their share of food aid for relief and emergency purposes.

Italian food aid policy

Italy has the third largest national food aid programme, and emphasises broad priorities in its policy. However, like the French programme, food aid for self-sufficiency is an objective and NGOs are not a major organisational means of disbursement of aid. The major form of giving food aid is on a government-to-government basis with the aid sold on recipients' markets and the counterpart funds used for both budgetary and balance of payments support. Italy, like France, also purchases its food on internal European markets, however Italian food aid is less dominated by cereals than that of France. Table II shows that Italy in 1991 had, in ECU terms, a larger food aid programme than that of France, although Table I indicates that in volume terms cereals aid is greater in France than Italy. Both France and Italy measure the costs of their food aid purchases in CAP terms and this differs from the German estimation which is nearer to the full cost of the food provided as aid. Emergency food aid has increased in Italy, as is the case in France and Germany. There are greater similarities with French and Italian food aid policy than there is with German.

Dutch food aid policy

The national food aid policy of the Netherlands has favoured multilateral donations, particularly to the World Food Programme, although broad humanitarian objectives have characterised Dutch food aid policy. The Dutch programme does favour food aid support for the self-sufficiency objectives in recipient agriculture, however this has been moderated into a broader view more akin to the objective of self-reliance and within the context of food strategies. This view is similar to that held by Germany. Food aid policy is a supplement to broader food strategies and is seen as a means of alleviating adverse outcomes for the dire poor and vulnerable groups as a result of structural adjustment programmes and conditionalities of the Bretton Woods Institutions. The Dutch are supportive of NGOs with their food aid.

40

United Kingdom food aid policy

As the fifth largest cereals food aid contributor in 1990, the UK, as has already been mentioned, has not favoured food as a form of development aid. Her comparative contributions during the 1970s and 1980s of food aid has been sporadic and usually in response to food shortages, as in the early 1970s and the mid-1980s. The United Kingdom's position on food as a form of development assistance has, to say the least, been sceptical since 1967-70, when she did not participate in the second FAC. In some sense her involvement with food aid has been determined by a commitment to the WFP and to European policy. The UK has consistently favoured food as relief and emergency aid, and not primarily for development purposes. The UK has changed its general position on food aid as a development resource over the decades of the 1970s and 1980s, giving support to the WFP operations, but preferring that food aid be primarily concerned with emergency and relief objectives.

The potential price displacement effects on recipient economies and the trade effects of food aid have been major preoccupations with UK policy (see, for example, Mettrick (1969) and Maxwell (1989) *Independent Group on British Aid*, (1989). Of all the European national programmes, the UK is the most sceptical of food aid as a development resource and prefers that this form of aid be earmarked for relief and emergency purposes. NGOs, the International Emergency Food Reserve of the WFP and the Red Cross, are favoured channels for UK food aid. Food aid is regarded as less efficient than financial aid and the UK has no government-to-government support, nor does it have direct project or programme food aid.

Swedish food aid policy

As one of the newest members of the Union, Sweden, has a national food aid programme and policy that in volume terms (for cereals) in the period of the late 1980s and early 1990s at 113,000 tons is equivalent to the size of the contribution of the Netherlands or the United Kingdom (Shaw and Clay, 1994). Swedish food aid policy has a greater multilateral emphasis than the other national food aid policies of the Union, with the exception of Denmark and the Netherlands. Swedish Policy has favoured

41

multilateral donations through the WFP, and since the 1970s, 80% of the country's food aid has been given to the UN system. The remainder has been focused upon selected countries primarily for relief and emergency purposes; a small amount of food aid is given to NGOs. Swedish policy favours projects to promote rural and agricultural efficiency and development in recipient economies; however there is concern over food aid subsidising poor agricultural policies and practices. The Swedish Programme is concerned to support the UN system and the objective of multilateral food aid policy, namely it is project orientated, and these tend to be of the food-for-work type of project, settlement schemes or rehabilitation, education and nutritional projects. The accession of Sweden to the Union is likely to strengthen the multilateral features of European food aid policy.

Smaller national food aid policies

The smaller national food aid programmes, such as Denmark, are, in effect, purely multilateral and channelled through the WFP, and do not provide bilateral assistance. Belgium and Luxembourg have a small programme of bilateral aid in addition to their WFP donations. Ireland meets its FAC obligations through the WFP donations and also provides support to NGOs, and an occasional one-off programme to a specific country on a government-to-government basis, such as milk powder to Egypt in 1990. Spain has provided government-to-government assistance to a number of countries.

As is so often the case with food aid policy, the determining factors are as a result of events, rather than a pre-planned use of food as a development resource. The surplus disposal of the Americans PL 480 in the 1950s and 1960s was but one response to agricultural productivity and protection within the American economy. The American initiative with food aid as a means of surplus disposal led to the emergence through the FAC of European national food aid policies and a single Union food aid policy. Having established programmes on the basis of surplus production in the first instance, national programmes varied in their food aid policy focus. Those countries, such as France and Italy, still retain vestiges of the surplus disposal emphasis in their respective food aid programme. This is particularly evident in their encouragement of a self-sufficiency objective in the agricultural and food policies of the recipients of their aid. The Latin countries of the Union have a strong government-to-government element in their food aid policies.

The Netherlands and Germany have sought, through the broadening of their development strategies towards recipient countries, to break the historic link between the agricultural protection objective of self-sufficiency that produced unwanted surpluses; to the trade oriented food security concept of self-reliance in agricultural and food policy in developing countries. In the case of the German national food aid policy, the emphasis on trade through the support of triangular transactions has sought to encourage trade between countries and regions as a means of encouraging agricultural reform and self-reliance in the food supply.

The countries of Northern Europe, such as Denmark, Holland and Sweden, have favoured the approach of the UN system as embodied in the WFP and their national programmes are, in effect, multilateral. Where trade issues are still a part of food aid policy, the governments tend to favour programme government-to-government donations. The emergence of the world food crisis of the 1970s, the African food crisis of the 1980s, and the increased number of man-made disasters, civil wars and natural disasters, have profoundly affected the national food aid policies and programmes of the members of the Union.

Nearly all the bilateral programmes of the members of the Union, either through their multilateral contributions or directly to recipients, have moved away from food aid as a longer-term development resource to that of shorter-term emergency, relief and rehabilitation aid. Food security policy frameworks adopted, particularly by Germany, places food aid as one component in a range of policies that are designed to strengthen the overall agricultural and economic situation in developing countries. To this degree, the role of food as aid is not regarded as superior to financial or technical aid, and for that matter, macroeconomic support. The United Kingdom has increased its food aid, where appropriate, for emergency relief and rehabilitation but not as a development resource as such, and does regard food aid as inferior to financial aid for development purposes. In addition to supplying food to the UN system and the Red Cross, a number of European countries have increased their support for NGOs by providing food for their emergency relief efforts and their projects.

The national programmes of the European Union reflect a spectrum of policy emphasis which ranges from small project-oriented multilateral support to bilateral government-to-government programme food aid. However, the recent events in the post-cold war 1990s has seen an increase in the food security policy programmes of donors where food aid plays a part that is mindful of negative trade effects and the importance of rural, agricultural and food strategies in developing countries. Emergency and disaster relief has become a major feature in the European national programmes, with humanitarian objectives often taking precedence over developmental objectives. The trade concerns of food aid have, for the time being, assumed a lesser profile than in earlier decades; however the national programmes still retain residual trade concerns which will be discussed in the following Chapter. Elements of the national food aid policies are, of course, evident in the Community-wide Union food aid policy which are given consideration as a separate policy in Chapter Four.

Note

1

	1968/69	1969/70	1970/71
National Actions	734	698	682
Community Actions	301	337	353
Total	**1035**	**1035**	**1035 (thousand tonnes)**

3 Agricultural trade policy, European food aid and surplus disposal

The European involvement with food aid began in the late 1960s at the behest of the United States of America, as part of an international wheat agreement which was concerned to stabilise prices in the cereals market and to share the burden of the costs of world food aid supplies amongst cereals exporters and importers. Food aid policies and trade policies, particularly in the world cereals market, have been inextricably intertwined since the emergence of the United States' PL 480 Programme of the early 1950s. The world food aid policy of the 1950s and 1960s was American food aid policy, which in turn was an integral part of US agricultural trade policy. Concessional sales of food by the US on to world markets had increased demand for American agricultural produce, and had provided commodities as aid. This form of development assistance was monitored for its adverse trade effects, particularly where unfair competition, or dumping was suspected. The rules of the FAO Committee on Surplus Disposal were concerned with competition and orderly marketing, rather than an attempt to have a market-wide agreement on the quantities, or prices of the commodities supplied in the world cereals market. The principles of surplus disposal were rules designed to safeguard competition in cereals markets by drawing attention to excesses with food aid and concessional sales of wheat as a means of export dumping.

The International Wheat Agreement of 1967 attempted to address the question of cereal prices and the quantities of cereals that would be made available as a minimum quantity of world food aid supplies. The IWAs of 1967, and 1971 had hoped to place a floor on world cereals prices which, in the event of the 1970's rise in world commodity prices, proved to be unnecessary. The Food Aid Convention was also unable to realise its intended world food aid targets because of the rise in cereals prices.

The establishment of the Common Agricultural Policy (CAP) in 1962 with its protectionist objectives, had profound implications for American agricultural trade, particularly in the european market itself, but also for the world market as a whole. The United States, in pressing for a Food Aid Convention, within the International Wheat Agreement, was ensuring that its own surplus disposal practices, if adopted by its competitors, would be subject to scrutiny and ultimately agreement in subsequent wheat agreements. The surplus disposal element in the PL 480 Programme, namely its concessional sales policy, is still very much part of American food aid policy. For the Americans, food aid and agricultural trade are complementary policies; an EU food aid programme has the potential to undermine commercial agricultural trade and it is therefore to be considered in commodity-wide agreements.

3.1 European agricultural policy and the international cereals trade

At the trade policy level European food aid has not repeated the overt trade expansionist aspects that were evident in the United States food aid policy of the 1950s and 1960s. European food aid policy has gradually adopted an emphasis that complements its other major policy initiatives. The Common Agricultural Policy is represented in food aid policy, by an emphasis upon self-sufficiency as a desirable agriculture policy objective for recipients. The idea of economic integration amongst third world countries is championed by the European Community through its promotion of the Generalised System of Preferences (GSP) and through the Lomé Conventions. European food aid has developed into new initiatives and policy areas such as triangular transactions, strategic regional and security stock programmes, as well as broader food security policies. These approaches are favoured by the Community as a means to achieve economic development and liberalised trade through encouraging economic integration in the developing world (see Cathie,

1987 and 1988).

Table III
Food aid and the international trade in cereals 1969-85

(thousand tonnes)

	World Exports[1]	World Food Aid	Developing[3] Countries Imports[1]	USA Exports[1]	USA Food Aid	EEC Exports[1]	EEC Food Aid[2]
1969	97,929		29,455	32,551		17,021	1,035
1970	114,430	12,800	33,662	40,392	9,995	17,498	1,035
1971	119,017	12,700	36,662	36,046	8,922	16,491	1,035
1972	134,857	12,563	34,375	52,473	9,259	20,378	978
1973	165,084	10,109	47,718	82,407	7,025	23,957	986
1974	149,046	5,651	48,309	65,167	3,198	24,972	1,208
1975	157,849	8,373	52,874	74,120	4,712	25,917	1,413
1976	166,150	6,856	49,640	81,010	4,284	21,434	928
1977	170,321	9,107	51,560	75,814	6,147	21,136	1,131
1978	191,574	9,216	75,202	93,968	5,992	26,848	1,374
1979	198,396	9,485	84,107	103,050	6,237	28,128	1,159
1980	222,505	8,887	97,757	112,906	5,418	34,182	1,205
1981	235,285	8,942	100,106	113,396	5,212	40,178	1,292
1982	221,662	9,140	100,033	100,603	5,341	36,193	1,602
1983	224,421	9,198	108,639	98,066	5,374	38,440	1,596
1984	236,671	9,831	112,338	103,754	5,655	45,488	1,917
1985	223,114	12,463	98,483	80,246	7,535	48,580	2,504

[1]   Food Aid included
[2]   Member States included
[3]   1969-1977 excludes China and planned Asian economies
Source: Henze et al (1982). See also FAO *Trade Year Books* 1980-1985 and FAO *Food Aid in Figures*, 1986.

Unlike United States food aid policy, European food aid policy does not pursue its commercial agricultural trade interest by providing concessional sales of food aid. The European Commission provides its food aid for emergency and developmental uses and these are in the form of grants.

Triangular transactions, for example, involve both commodity aid and cash aid to promote economic integration. European food aid policy in the 1980s has decoupled from its commercial trade interests and it is questionable whether its food aid was ever entirely seen in Brussels as an agricultural trade development instrument. Table III shows the position of food aid and the international trade in cereals from 1969 to 1985. World cereals exports have more than doubled during the period, but world food aid fell from its high in 1970 (in volume terms) only to return to 12 million tonnes in 1985.

Throughout the period, in volume terms, grain exports steadily increased as markets developed, but food aid declined relative to the world market growth. The concessional element in agricultural trade deals, including food aid deals, fell from 18% of world trade in 1970 to 4% in 1985 (see Cathie, 1985). The world market in grains moved during the 1970s to a position where price policy was playing a greater part in determining market share and growth, an experience that had not been seen since the 1920s.

During the 1970s, the market growth in cereals was strongest in developing countries where in volume terms this increased by a factor of three. Periodically during the 1970s, Soviet and Chinese purchases helped to keep world market demand buoyant. However, these segments of the market were erratic and unpredictable, whereas developing country growth is not. It is anticipated by some experts that the future growth prospects in the cereals market lie in the developing countries (see, for example, Mellor and Johnston, 1984).

United States food aid has declined throughout the period and the relationship between American commercial export interests and food aid has been established (see Hopkins, 1983). Hopkins has shown that United States food aid policy is correlated with United States agricultural wheat surpluses throughout nearly all of the period (1955-1977). As food aid declined, so commercial trade expanded. Food aid and concessional sales had developed markets, and as these were secured for commercial trade, so food aid volumes declined. Food aid was not used to the same degree as an instrument of commercial and trade expansion in the 1970s, as it had been in the 1950s and 1960s.

Figure 2 shows the relationship between world wheat food aid and world prices during the period 1971-90. Clay and Benson (1993) found,

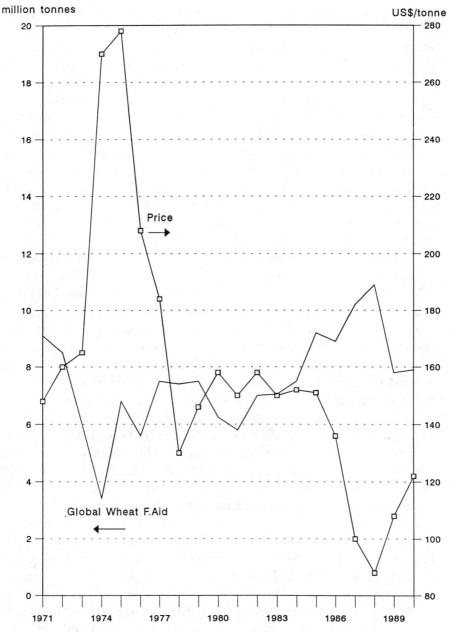

Figure 2 Movements in Global Wheat Food Aid and World Prices 1971-89

Note: Marketing year = July 1970-June1971 etc.

Source: ODI, Clay and Benson, 1993

using a simple linear regression, a negative relationships between prices and volumes of wheat aid. Given that the US is still the premier wheat food aid exporter, the trend set by the changes in US agricultural trade policy from 1970 is discernable in global food aid policy during the 1970s and 1980s. The period of the so-called World Food Crisis marked a major change in the world cereals market as it saw the re-establishment of the price mechanism in determining supplies. The overall availability of cereals supplies for food aid were reduced and those supplies that were available were on terms that were more market price determined. The concessional elements in food aid donations were harder for recipients. The surplus capacities both in stockholdings and general supply of wheat as aid had been permanently reduced and American agricultural exports were focused upon markets as commercial opportunities. The situation of food aid as a counter-cyclical activity on the behalf of global donors is not indicated in the relationship between the price of wheat and the volumes of wheat available as food aid.

The major wheat exporters and food aid donors were the USA and Canada and their contribution to world supplies dominates the pro-cyclical nature of prices of wheat and the supply of wheat as food aid. The relationship reinforces the view that the Food Aid Convention is concerned, in the main, with a residual to the commercial agricultural trade situation and the inclusion of surplus disposal within the broader aims of commercial agricultural trade policy rather than meeting global food aid targets. The liberalisation of agricultural trade rules under the Uruguay Round of the GATT furthers the possibility of this pro-cyclical relationship of prices and volumes of cereals being maintained and even made more acute. As the supply of food aid is channelled more in the direction of humanitarian and relief aid, so the relationship between surplus disposal for developmental purposes and international markets and prices is broken.

The period of the 1970s and 1980s still indicates that surplus disposal and its effects on exporters' trade prospects is a concern with the major food aid donor, the United States. Food aid, where it is supplied for humanitarian and relief purposes, that is to say distributed as a grant for specified periods and to deal with particular natural or man-made disasters, does not pose a threat to commercial agricultural activities either on the world market or, for that matter, within recipient countries.

The pro-cyclical nature of prices and volumes of food aid indicates that the major donors' belief in food aid as means of providing resources for the development of recipient economies has not been generally maintained during the 1970s and 1980s.

This global picture contrasts with the largely US experience of the 1950s' and 1960s' surplus utilisation of excess supplies for the economic development of recipients such as South Korea, and indicates a counter-cyclical relationship between supplies and prices. The South Korean economy benefitted through a certainty of supplies (effectively given as outright grants) with budgetary aid, balance of payments support as well as a direct support to the wage good in that industrialising economy (see Cathie, 1989).

The EU wheat food aid and world prices during the period 1971-90 contrasts with that of global wheat food aid. Clay and Benson (1993) found that there was no positive or negative relationship between either total European food aid, or Community actions with regard to wheat aid and international market prices. The relationship, as shown in Figure 3, does differ from that shown in Figure 2, and may reflect the steady growth and the maintenance of European wheat supplies as aid. However, the effects of the CAP on world wheat supplies and prices has perhaps dampened the tendencies of the pro-cyclical relationship between prices and food supplies that are determined by US and Canadian food aid policies. The EU, of course, has increased its surplus during the 1970s and 1980s and these supplies have, to some degree, substituted for American and Canadian supplies, as the Americans have intended with the Food Aid Convention.

Some of the burden of world food aid costs were being assumed by the Union during the 1970s and 1980s, but European food aid policy has not followed a counter-cyclical policy any more than the Americans have. Member States of the Union such as the UK, who don't have structural surpluses of wheat, do not have an identifiable relationship between their food aid programmes and prices. However, Clay and Benson did find a significant negative relationship between the volume of French wheat food aid and the world price. France, after the US and Canada, is the world's third largest exporter of wheat.

France has followed a bilateral food aid policy that in some respects is nearer to that of the United States' food policy than any other member

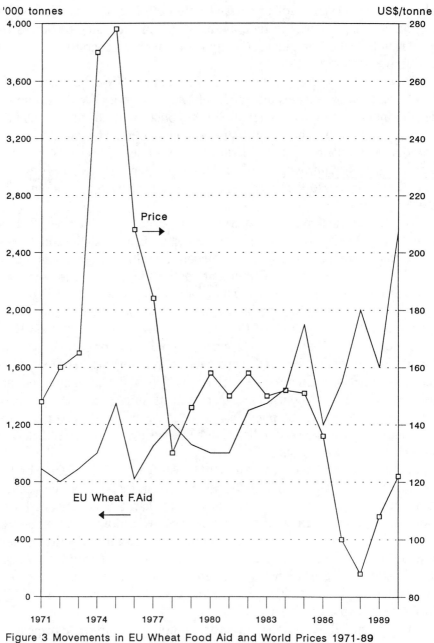

'000 tonnes   US$/tonne

Price

EU Wheat F.Aid

Figure 3 Movements in EU Wheat Food Aid and World Prices 1971-89
Note: Marketing year = July 1970-June1971 etc.
Source: ODI, Clay and Benson, 1993

states of the Union. The disposal of surplus French agricultural commodities is sustained by the pricing policy of the Common Agricultural Policy and its own bilateral food aid policy. The French see their agricultural trade policy and food aid policy as one element in their foreign and commercial policy. The French influence on European Union food aid policy has not caused Europe to try and replicate the trade and aid emphasis of PL 480, although French policy is concerned with commercial markets for its agricultural produce and it is also concerned with food aid as a means not only to aid recipients, but also to create agricultural export markets, in ways other member states are not. French food aid (as was noted in Chapter Two) is given in considerable quantity to countries with commercial potential, such as Egypt, as well as other countries in Africa where there are Francophone interests, both commercial and political. The American concern with the potential for European food aid undermining commercial markets is perhaps more focused upon French food aid policy than it is upon Community-wide food aid policy.

The European Community has steadily expanded its cereals food aid throughout the period, with the years 1972, 1973 and 1976 dropping below one million tonnes. The EEC has doubled its food aid in the period to over two million tonnes in 1985, whereas the United States has not again reached its 1970 donations. European trade in cereals has grown three-fold during the period, while food aid has doubled. European food aid is not proportionate to the European cereals trade and the relationship between food aid and market development is not as strong as is the case with the United States. The development in food aid policy and in market developments suggests that the EEC, consistent with its own policy, precepts and principles, is not using its food aid policy as an instrument of trade development. Dieter Frisch, Director-General for development, in 1989, correctly noted that there is no recognisable correlation between Community surpluses and its food aid (Courier, no.118, December 1989).

In some ways this is a surprising conclusion, since the United States is constantly accusing the European Community of undermining United states markets in Europe and the developing world. While the growth in European exports (Table III) includes intra-trade, that is the trade between EEC members; it is perhaps in this area of the market that the United States feels justified in complaining about unfair trade practice, although

Table IV
The European export trade in cereals 1969-85

(thousand tonnes)*

	1969	1970	1971	1972	1973	1974	1975	1976	1977	1978	1979	1980	1981	1982	1983	1984	1985
Belgium/Luxembourg	743	887	719	1,128	1,020	976	2,038	2,094	2,053	2,030	3,084	3,367	3,590	3,603	3,242	4,246	3,166
Denmark	405	351	228	339	352	668	1,013	592	704	1,363	1,020	1,139	542	725	873	1,492	1,549
France	12,293	10,284	11,532	14,454	16,294	17,530	13,229	14,020	11,012	14,762	16,987	19,637	22,125	19,379	23,078	25,681	28,717
FR Germany	1,572	2,838	1,441	1,961	2,444	1,986	1,825	2,393	2,392	2,024	1,989	2,414	2,485	2,411	2,512	3,365	2,613
Greece	0	0	0	0	0	0	0	0	0	0	0	765	591	986	1,284	1,535	942
Ireland	3	4	2	2	63	60	72	68	74	346	222	246	109	1,688	149	254	297
Italy	547	1,386	1,072	1,002	873	727	1,161	849	946	1,185	1,716	1,845	2,222	2,557	1,872	1,953	3,332
Netherlands	1,430	1,478	1,376	1,406	2,547	2,770	5,152	1,023	3,157	2,622	2,011	1,660	1,817	1,132	1,010	1,148	1,238
Portugal	0	1	8	6	7	4	8	9	0	0	0	5	6	3	2	6	3
Spain	0	0	0	0	0	0	0	0	0	0	0	305	1,943	341	498	160	1,496
United Kingdom	28	269	121	84	362	251	1,442	386	800	2,516	1,099	2,799	4,745	4,887	3,920	6,168	5,031
Total EEC	17,021	17,498	16,492	20,379	23,957	24,972	25,918	21,435	21,137	26,849	28,128	34,183	40,173	36,193	38,440	45,489	48,389

* (this includes intra and inter European Trade)

Source: FAO *Trade Year Books* 1971-1985.

one would have to completely discount the theory of economic integration as a means to measure these criticisms as being justified. In the sphere of food aid policy the United States would not have a justifiable claim that the EEC were using this policy as an instrument of market development. Perhaps the United states is assessing European food aid policy in terms of its own food aid policy experience, rather than assessing it in European terms, and in terms that independently would justify a claim.

3.2   The European trade in cereals

The European trade in cereals has risen from 17 million tonnes in 1969 to over 48 million tonnes in 1985, increasing its world market share considerably (Tables III, p.47 and IV p.54). Table IV shows that France has more than doubled its trade in cereals throughout the period and it is the dominant cereals trader in the EEC. This dominance may be greater than is reflected in the figures, since because of EEC restitutions and other subsidies, French grain may additionally be trans-shipped through the Belgian and Dutch ports. Table IV indicates a larger volume of grain exported from Belgium, Luxembourg and the Netherlands than is likely from their production potential. These countries may be showing their traditional entrepôt trade in addition to their cereals production increase. The aggregate figures of the European export trade do contain an element of double counting, for the reasons given, and therefore some care is required in analysing them.

Like France, both Italy and Germany show a steady growth in their respective cereals trade. The United Kingdom since 1981 has shown a stronger propensity to export. However, before this date, UK cereals trade appears to be the weakest of all the European cereals producers.

This situation may result from a reluctance to realise the changing underlying basis for European agricultural trade and the traditional position of the United Kingdom as a net importer of cereals. While the United Kingdom is a member of the European agricultural community and takes part in its policy formulation, it is possible that it has been unable to fully discard its atavistic adherence to nineteenth century liberalism. Of course, on this adherence the United Kingdom has more in common with the United States than it does with its trading partners in continental

Europe. In this sense it could be said to be the least agricultural export-trade conscious member of the EEC: where agricultural trade is in the United Kingdom a passive instrument of trade policy, in the rest of Europe it is an active instrument of policy. An example of the United Kingdom's passive agricultural trade policy would be in a reluctance to give credits for expansion, and the agencies concerned have a low profile on export promotion.

Table V gives the net of intra-European trade in the cereals sector and shows that wheat and coarse grains have doubled during the period 1969-1986, and that wheat alone has increased by a factor of three. This world market growth of cereals for the EEC, taken together with the growth in the internal trade market, clearly shows the basis for American fears for maintaining her market share in the world cereals market. United states policy has sought, successfully through the GATT Uruguay Round, to promote a liberalisation of agricultural trade policy. Agricultural trade policy has been adopted into the rules of the new World Trade Organisation (WTO) which is the successor to the GATT.

The market for American agricultural produce in Europe has been affected by the enlargement of the Community as the Common Agricultural Policy has continued to exclude competitive access. The effects of the enlarged European market on United States agricultural exports, particularly in the 1970s and 1980s, have to be differentiated from providing food aid to food deficit developing countries. It is perhaps the systematic exclusion of the United States from the European market and the development of the internal European agricultural market itself that concerns the United States rather than the food aid policy of the Community.

Community agricultural trade policy with regard to cereals appears to have broken the link with food aid policy as an instrument of market development during the years 1975-86. While world food aid volumes reduced during the 1970s, EEC volumes stabilised, making its donations second to those of the United States. Whereas the United States food aid policy developed in line with its commercial market development aims, European food aid policy has not sought its own agricultural trade development, although French bilateral food aid policy has a closer link with its own commercial market development. As a consequence of this different approach to surplus disposal, the Europeans have not used food

Table V
EEC exports of wheat and coarse grain 1969-85

	(million tonnes)	
	Wheat and Coarse Grain	Wheat Only
	(excludes intra-EC Trade)	
1969	12.5	5.6
1970	9.0	3.6
1971	8.2	3.8
1972	10.1	5.1
1973	10.5	5.0
1974	10.7	6.9
1975	13.0	8.6
1976	9.0	5.1
1977	10.5	5.0
1978	14.3	8.8
1979	15.7	10.4
1980	21.6	14.7
1981	19.7	15.5
1982	20.6	15.6
1983	19.7	15.4
1984	27.0	18.1
1985	23.7	17.0

Source: FAS/USDA, various issues.

aid policy for trade expansion but have attempted, as they claim, to give food as a development resource and to encourage the development of the indigenous agricultural sector of recipients of its aid.

The surplus disposal of Union cereals to the developing world is not designed to increase European agricultural trade. Cereals food aid is given in the form of grants not sold concessionally, and it is given to a large number of developing countries in relatively small quantities, and often at irregular intervals. Increasingly, Union food aid is given as humanitarian and relief assistance which, by its very nature, is sporadic and relatively short-term. The supply of food aid to areas of natural and man-made disaster, and to low income countries are, by definition, unlikely to be future commercial markets for European produce. Cereals aid is, however, rising as a proportion of overall European food aid as the supply of commodities, such as skimmed milk powder, have been reduced.

The Common Agricultural Policy with its pricing policy, its levels of protection and its export restitutions, have a distortionary affect upon the world cereals market and particularly upon the prices of cereals. In the absence of the CAP it has been argued that world prices would be significantly different from what they have been with European protection. Cereal prices and overall output would increase for the world as a whole and the instability of supply would be reduced with agricultural liberalisation (World Development Report, 1986). The Common Agricultural Policy adds to food insecurity by its potential to destabilise world cereals markets, in a similar way that the United States' Agricultural Policy prior to 1970s depressed world prices with concessional sales and massive stock overhangs.

The destabilising effects on world markets of the Common Agricultural Policy are not offset by Community food aid policy, since major recipients of European food aid are only a selective few countries who regularly receive this form of European aid. Food aid, whether European or not, is not as reliable a source of the food supply as are world markets, since food aid allocations are determined *inter alia* by developmental consideration, by bureaucratic inertia, supply availability and political considerations.

The experience of Botswana, for example, with the supply of food aid for her food security programme, indicates that food aid is the least reliable means of obtaining her food security objectives when compared with international markets and prices (Cathie and Dick, 1987). European food aid was a significant part of the overall supplies of food aid to that country, although these supplies varied not according to her food needs but were determined by the supplies made available by the donors. The irregularity of supplies of food aid by Europe to many developing countries, taken together with the relatively small amounts of food aid available, suggests that the developmental contribution is not significant.

While the Union food aid policy is not explicitly concerned with using food aid for the development of European agricultural markets, the Common Agricultural Policy adds uncertainty and instability to the world cereals market. This effect of the CAP in turn adds to world food insecurity and prevents poor countries that do not receive European food aid from the benefits of liberalised agricultural trade. Those who do receive European food aid are also not necessarily compensated for the price depressing and supply effects of the CAP.

European food aid is costed in terms of CAP prices which are higher than prevailing world prices, and to this extent Union food aid bears the higher costs of the CAP. European food aid is not costed at world prices but at higher European costs. In 1991-92 the EU programme food aid (including national programmes) in wheat to fifteen recipients, with three exceptions, were at costs in excess of commercial import costs. Other commodities, such as vegetable oil, skimmed milk powder and rice, were also higher than alternative commercial costs. If Union food aid were costed at world market prices, then the value of the food aid would be lower on average than it in fact appears to be. The issue of how to value food aid, of course, is not a new one. Schultz (1963) in his famous article on PL 480, estimated that the value of that aid at that time was as little as 30% of the nominal value of the aid stated by the Commodity Credit Corporation (CCC). These European Union costs being much higher than world market prices, reflect the higher costs of the CAP.

If European food aid costs are given at triangular transactions costs, such as with Tanzania and Mozambique, then these costs are nearer to those on regional, or world markets than the costs of obtaining the food within the Union. In so far as triangular transactions are promoted within national food aid programmes, such as that of Germany and within the Union itself, these purchases not only promote trade between developing countries but also narrow the gap between higher cost CAP procured food for aid and costs in non-protected markets. The question of food aid being substituted for financial aid becomes less of a problem when the procurement costs from a protected market and an unprotected market are narrower than when they can be as much as 92% greater than alternative commercial supplies.

The magnitude of difference between European food aid and alternative commercial sources and the quantities of commodities supplied to those recipients, with few exceptions, could have been procured with finance at much lower cost. European food aid in cost terms is therefore in a similar position to that of the US in the 1960s, in that it is overvalued and its benefits to the recipient should be discounted in relation to alternative commercial supplies. The use of triangular transactions as a means of food aid procurement provides the opportunity for the Union to measure its food aid costs to recipients as actual market costs, as opposed to CAP costs.

Dairy aid was the first commodity introduced to the Union after the cereals FAC agreement in 1967, and was the beginning of a widening of commodities available within the European programme, and it was also the exclusive policy of the Union as opposed to national programmes. Dairy aid has been a particularly controversial form of European food aid for a number of reasons. At the international level, dairy aid in its origins in the Common Agricultural Policy, is surplus to European market demand, and its use as aid is the disposal of a surplus. In this sense it is similar in many ways to PL 480 in the 1950s and 1960s, although the dairy aid is given as a grant and not sold concessionally. Dairy aid has, in value terms over the 1980s, been as much as 40-60% of Union food aid costs, in short half the value of the European food aid programme has been taken by Dairy aid (Maxwell, 1990 in *Real Aid*).

The size, and particulary the value, of European food aid attributable to dairy aid and its direct linking with CAP policies has encouraged the view that the purpose of this aid is export dumping. The impact on recipient economies of dairy aid, particularly the large scale European programme to India 'Operation Flood', is still subject to controversy as to its effectiveness as a form of aid. India has received EU dairy aid for twenty-five years continuously, and during the last ten years has been subject to severe criticism from the Court of Auditors within the Union itself (in 1988), and from numerous academic analysts (Doornbos, Gertsch and Terhal, 1991). In a direct response to this criticism of dairy aid the Community has in the 1980s reduced its overall supplies. Dairy aid is still, however, a major feature of the European programme and will be discussed further in Chapter Six. The United States has doubled its SMP food aid in the ten years since 1979, and in quantity terms exceeds that of the Union. However, the distinction between concessional sales and grants of dairy aid have to be borne in mind when assessing the surplus disposal of the dairy commodities and market development. The

EU, while disposing of its surpluses, has not created new markets for European produce. At least this has been the case with Operation Flood until the present time.

European Union food aid policy has not sought commercial market development as an objective of its policy, nor has it sought to discourage trade in agricultural markets of recipients, as the United States has done with its PL 480 Programme (Cathie, 1990). PL 480 in prohibiting recipients of its food aid from trade in the 'same as commodities' given as food aid. Countries receiving say wheat, under PL 480, could not export home grown wheat as a condition of the food aid agreement. This stricture discourages trade in recipient countries, and to that extent was anti-trade in its bias. The European union, through its promotion of triangular transactions, adopted from WFP Policy and its commitments to the Food Aid Convention, has introduced a pro-trade influence into its food aid and food security policies. The United States has not used triangular transactions to the same extent that the EU has in its food aid policy.

Food aid policy and its effects on international agricultural trade, particularly the fears of its use as a rationalisation for export dumping and surplus disposal, are present in the watchdog roles of the Committee on surplus disposals and the monitoring of food aid transactions by, amongst others, the OECD, the FAO, and the FAC of the International Wheat Agreements. The European food aid policy that has evolved in the 1970s and 1980s has been less overtly concerned with expanding its own markets by creating commercial markets in developing countries than by developing policies for the use of food as aid and, in addition, developing policies for food strategies within developing countries who are recipients of its aid. The following Chapter will discuss the policy framework and the management of European Community food aid and related policies.

4 The formulation and management of European Union food aid policies and programmes 1968-1994

4.1 The emergence of European food aid policy and related trade and aid policies

The European Community food aid programmes and policies began in a pragmatic and almost half-hearted way in response to an agricultural trade issue with regard to the world cereals market, and particularly in response to a request from the United States to spread the burden of world food aid costs and supplies amongst the industrial agricultural exporters and importers of cereals. European Union food aid policy was haphazard in its conception and its commitment was to a particular share of the overall Food Aid Convention target for world food aid. The Community began its programme with one commodity, cereals and a generally broad framework in which it saw where food aid might provide assistance to developing countries.

The Consultative Assembly of the Council of Europe of the Organisation for Economic Co-operation and Development (OECD) in 1964 had passed Resolution 270 on Food Aid, this being the first attempt to formulate a particular OECD position on the role of this form of development assistance. The resolution sought to distinguish between surplus disposal as an outcome of agricultural protection and food aid as a form of development assistance. Food aid programmes should be designed for the needs of the receiving country and not for the adaption of surplus producing countries agricultural policy. The newly established multilateral programme of the FAO/WFP in 1963 was to carry out studies that could indicate how food aid might contribute to economic development without delaying agricultural development, and in addition to emergency relief and social welfare. The Assembly endorsed the Freedom from Hunger Campaign (FFHC) of the FAO which aimed to promote policies which would attempt to raise agricultural production in the less developing countries.

The European Community and its members having accepted this OECD Resolution, had also accepted the broad principles in which its own programme established, three years after this Resolution, would operate. Resolution 270, in distinguishing between surplus disposal and food aid, sought to break the link between agricultural protection and export dumping. For the Community, food aid was not to be an instrument of commercial agricultural policy for the purposes of market enlargement and agricultural trade promotion. In accepting this Resolution 270, prior to the establishment of its own programme, the Union had undertaken to accept that food aid and surplus disposal should not be linked in its own operations. Resolution 270 also pointed towards support for the multilateral food aid experiments of the World Food Programme as the basis for a European programme. The early EEC food aid programme from 1968 until 1971 channelled Community food aid through the WFP and therefore it was argued that European policy was multilateral in its character. In 1970 the Union added skimmed milk powder (SMP), butteroil, egg products and sugar to its list of commodities for use as food aid, and the WFP was the original channel for Operation Flood, the Dairy aid programme to India.

The European Community has grown from a Customs Union concerned with the harmonisation of non-agricultural trade policy to add further areas of common policy since 1958. The European idea has involved building upon both the Customs Union and a common internal policy for agriculture as the original key common policies for integration. The Treaty of Rome however, did contain other elements of broader policy concern such as social provisions within the Community (particularly within the CAP), but also for aid relations with developing countries that had historic associations with Community countries. The European idea has involved the framework of the *acquis communitaire* which has incorporated the major treaties of the Community, from the original European Coal and Steel Community, Euratom, the Treaty of Rome, the

Common Agricultural Policy; the enlargements of the 1970s, 1980s and 1990s, the Exchange Rate Mechanism (ERM) and European Monetary System (EMS), the Single European Act of the 1980s, and the Maastricht Agreement of the 1990s. The *acquis communitaire*, in addition to the internal European agreements, also incorporates European agreements with the rest of the world through the GATT, the IMF and the World Bank as well as the wider Agreements with the UN system (Tsoukalis, 1993).

The process of economic integration has also involved political integration in so far as a common European policy has gradually emerged in areas that have wider implications than economic matters alone. European relations with the developing world and the emergent economies in particular, have seen the evolution of policies towards Mediterranean countries; the Transitional economies, Latin America and Asia, all of which attempt to frame a European-wide policy towards these areas and regions.

The progress towards complete economic and political integration has involved the building of the *acquis communitaire,* providing the framework for economic and political deepening and successive enlargements of the Union. Both of these broad categories, deepening and enlargement, have produced tensions within the Union and with the rest of the world over the period since the Community was first established in the 1950s. Community policy has balanced between forms of protectionism as part of the integration process and freer, more liberalised trade policy. The European Union is, however, along with the greater part of the world economy, more liberalised than was the case in the 1950s. The European Community has had a common trade policy within the Customs Union arrangements, and also as a consequence of the Common Agricultural Policy, common agricultural trade arrangements with the rest of the world.

The industrial, commercial and agricultural trade policies of the Union have been subject to major changes over time through international trade agreements which have involved a greater integration of the economies within the members of the Union and with the rest of the world. This process of economic deepening has been both gradual and continuous over the period since the Treaty of Rome in 1958. The enlargements of the Union have also been accompanied by additions to policy over and above the idea of the original Customs Union with its common trade policy. The Treaty of Rome and its protocols had made provision for the retention, or the setting up of special relationships with what was, in effect, former colonies of the original EEC members. These provisions were the beginnings of both a common trade and aid policy towards developing countries which began to be formulated in detail during the 1960s. The Common Agricultural Policy was also established in 1962 with its specific objectives and instruments of policy being detailed, and with its specific implications for developing countries on access to European markets for their agricultural produce.

The Community had recognised in the first Yaoundé Convention in 1963 that the partnership with specific developing countries would place trade with these countries at the centre of its arrangements for development co-operation. The EEC had, through its policy of a common approach towards developing countries with respect to trade and aid, began to widen its policy beyond that of a Customs Union towards a European-wide policy that was inevitably distinctive from the sum of all the national aid policies of the member states. Aid and trade policy taken together with commercial and defence policy constitute the instruments of foreign policy of a nation state, and the Treaty of Rome contained provision for aid as well as that of its common trading policy. The United States had linked its food aid policy and development policy through PL 480; and through its Mutual Security Acts PL 665, PL 82-165, PL 83-77 and PL 83-266; all providing food surpluses as military aid (see Cathie, 1989 and Wallerstein, 1980).

The United States has used food aid as a major instrument to pursue its foreign policy goals, from its early use in lend-lease programmes, during the Marshall Plan period in Europe and with PL480 being given to over 130 developing countries. PL480 played a major role in providing US aid to Vietnam, as well as providing food aid to both Israel and Egypt as part of the Camp David settlement of the Arab-Israeli conflict. The European Union, through its trade and aid policies, has developed a surrogate European foreign policy that is separate and co-exists with each of the member state's own foreign policy objectives, but it is not completed without defence policy. Europe has been able to find common ground with trade and aid policy towards developing countries and in its dealings with OECD countries and particularly with trade negotiations in the GATT.

The European Union has, however, been unable to reach common ground with regard to a common foreign policy where the issue of a common defence position is required, such as the situation in the former Yugoslavia and the Balkans. Union policy has not superseded national members' own policies towards developing countries but it has provided a framework for the convergence of national policies and an addition to these national policies. Both European aid and trade policies are by no means completely harmonised, and national policies towards developing countries diverge from that of the Union policy. A recent example of the divergence is that of the Banana Protocol of the Lome Agreement which had given preferential access to European markets to African Carribean and Pacific (ACP) banana producers. The Banana Protocol has had to be phased out because of the Single European Act which requires a Community-wide common import policy which must take precedence over the banana protocol. Both Germany and the Netherlands pressed for the removal of preferential access to the Union of the Caribbean banana producers over those lower cost non-ACP producers from Latin America.

The second Yaoundé Convention was agreed in 1969, together with the Arusha Agreement, also in 1969. This was followed in 1971 by the Generalised System of Preferences (GSP) which covered almost all industrial products and some processed agricultural products, and gave preferential access to European markets as a principle of development co-operation to developing county members in association with the EEC.

The Community concept of Associationism had been introduced in the Treaty of Rome (articles 131-36 Part IV) by France who wanted to ensure free access to the Community of exports from her former colonies (see Grilli, 1994). Germany and the Netherlands agreed to this Gallic notion. However, they preferred an emphasis on development co-operation that applied to all developing countries, not just associates of France, Belgium and Italy, the former colonial powers. Associationism in the Treaty of Rome created a free trade area between the EEC and the States of their dependencies and amongst the dependencies themselves. The Treaty of Rome established a collective responsibility of member states to provide financial assistance (foreign aid) and free trade with those developing countries in association with the Community. The European Development Fund (EDF) was established to provide Community resources to supplement the bilateral aid programmes of the member states to the associates of the EEC.

In 1971, European aid policy adopted the Generalised System of Preferences (GSP) at the behest of the United Nations Conference on Trade and Development (UNCTAD). This covered almost all industrial products and some processed agricultural products. The GSP allowed preferential access from associate members into the European market. European aid policy consolidated in 1975 with the first Lome Convention, where the group of developing countries was enlarged and given the acronym of ACP (Africa, Caribbean, Pacific countries).

The Lome Convention has been extended through four agreements: 1975-79, 1980-84, 1985-89, 1990-2000. Each of these agreements has refined and extended the basic notion of Associationism with the EU. In 1958 there were 55 million people in Associate countries; however, by 1990 the number of countries in Association had increased such that the ACP country population reached 493 million. Total aid had been half a billion ECU in 1958, and by 1990 12 billion ECU was provisioned under Lome IV (Courier No. 120, March 1990). The EU aid programme had added instruments of policy such as specific funds for the stabilisation of certain commodity exports from Associate countries and the GSP. Associationism, however, was essentially the provision of free access to EU markets and aid to the ACP countries. The Lome Agreements have, however, come under continuing criticism from the ACP countries themselves, on the grounds that the funds available from the Union are insufficient to meet their development needs. Lome IV negotiations with the ACP countries proved difficult, and some critics of the Union policy have argued that the European aid and trade initiatives embodied in Lome I-III have run out of steam in Lome IV during the 1990s (see Grilli, 1994).

Lome IV may have, in the 1990s, reached the limit for European Associationism because of the end of the cold war which has placed pressure on the EU to help the Eastern European countries with economic reforms and democratic development. Many of the Eastern European countries look to free access to European markets and membership of the Community as a means of consolidating their economic and political freedoms. Fifteen of the seventy Lome country members have been either suspended, or have had their concessions reduced because their governments are judged by the Union to be undemocratic, i.e. Nigeria, Zaire and the Sudan. There is also widespread 'donor fatigue' in the western world, including the EU. The Lome Conventions have provided since 1975 some 30 billion ECUs, with very meagre results in terms of the economic performance of the recipient economies. Lome has been unable to accommodate post-apartheid South Africa into full membership of that agreement since that economy is judged to be too advanced in parts for special access to the EU markets. However, the agreement as it stands to 2,000 will benefit the farm exports of som of the Lome members (see *Economist*, November 1995).

The food aid policy of the Union is not funded through the Lome Agreements although the Lome Convention IV does contain a broad statement of European food aid policy (article 51) as but one facet of the trade and aid relationship with ACP countries. This statement is in the form of a general provision for food aid. European food aid policy is not, however, exclusive to ACP countries and indeed it has been argued that the Lome countries do not receive a disproportionate share of European food aid compared with non-associated countries (Clay and Benson 1993). Some of the European Union's major recipients such as Egypt, India and Bangladesh, not to mention the Eastern European countries who have received large quantities of Union food aid since 1990, are not Lome members.

While European Union food aid is part of overall Union aid policy, it is not embedded within the purpose of the Lome Conventions, and indeed this policy of commodity aid was conceived separately from the particular aid and trade policies that are central to Associationism. European food aid policy has a much wider significance as a policy than Lome, which is designed for Associate members of the Community, since it grants aid to developing countries in general and as such has widened the Union's aid activities towards the Third World in general, and the emerging transitional economies in particular. Food aid policy, while forming part of Associationism, also goes beyond it, and adds to the Union's broader nascent foreign policy objectives. Food aid in the form of humanitarian aid allows the Community not only to pursue humanitarian objectives but also to provide assistance in areas such as Africa, the Balkans and Northern Iraq where there are European foreign policy interests.

The European Union does not have a fully developed foreign policy position apart from its trade policy core of the Customs Union and its unified negotiated position under the former GATT, and now with the WTO. The Maastricht Treaty, however, does make provision for a common foreign and security policy which will be developed as the detail of the treaty framework is agreed within Europe, namely through the inter-governmental meeting in 1996 and also in agreements between the Council of Ministers, the Commission and the European Parliament. This trade position is, however, subject to strong national policy influences and differences, particularly with the Common Agricultural Policy where the United Kingdom holds its historic position of free trade for agriculture and is in favour of reforming, or even dismantling the CAP. France takes the view that the Common Agricultural Policy is a pillar of European policy and is as important to European unity as is the customs union and the policy harmonisations of the single market and the Maastricht Agreement. The other members of the Union hold views on the CAP that fall between the dirigisme of France and the *laissez-faire* of the UK. Germany, while supporting the CAP, is also a strong supporter of free-trade.

The European Union's nascent foreign policy position in trade and aid towards the developing world emphasises Associationism with ACP countries, specific policies towards the Mediterranean countries of the Mashreg and Magreb Regions, Latin America and the transitional economies of Eastern Europe, as well as South Asia. The EU has given trade concessions, especially to the ACP countries, that appear to have a greater coherence than its concessions to the Mediterranean countries, Latin America, South Asia or the transitional economies of Eastern Europe. The CAP has proved a problem in the Union dialogue with the Mediterranean countries, and Latin America, and is likely to be so with the transitional economies of Eastern Europe (Grilli, 1994).

The Union's policy in trade and aid towards the developing world taken as a whole represents a fragmented series of surrogate foreign policy objectives, and as the Community has increased in its own membership and size, it has become more difficult to maintain an overall coherence. Food aid policy straddles EU aid policies towards the developing world taken as a whole and includes the transitional economies of Eastern Europe. Food aid policy is not a product of Associationism, nor is it strictly a part of Union trade policy; it was a reaction in the first instance to outside pressure to ensure that the surplus capacity of the CAP did not become a feature of European aid policy.

From 1968 until the so-called World Food Crisis of 1974 the EU food aid policy evolved along multilateral lines, that is to say the community-wide policy favoured channelling its food aid mainly through the WFP, with some of its food aid going directly to the United Nations High Commission for Refugees (UNHCR) and the Red Cross. Community food aid policy was therefore influenced by the policies of the UN system which favoured project oriented food aid donations and a wide distribution of relatively small donations to a large number of developing countries. In its early years, channelling EEC food aid through the WFP avoided any potential conflict of policy between the Union and the policies of member states while allowing the Community-wide policy to be established. The EEC also broadened the basket of commodities that could be given through its programmes and began to channel food directly to recipients using its own operations.

4.2   EU food aid policy from the 1970s

Community food aid policy in 1974 had three broad categories for its operations, emergency assistance, nutritional objectives and operations for development. The emergency assistance focused upon the Sahel countries, victims of the Nigerian Civil War and Bengali refugees of the war between India and Pakistan. Nutritional operations were mainly through the United Nations Relief Works Administration (UNRWA) to Palestine refugees. Operations for development were aimed at foreign exchange savings from food aid imports, and where the aid was sold on their national markets, providing counterpart funds for the financing of development projects. The Commission published a Memorandum on Food Aid Policy of the EEC (Com (74) 300 Final) to the European Council of Ministers, in which it argued for a coherent Community-wide food aid policy while acknowledging that food aid was not a satisfactory permanent solution to the food problems of developing countries.

The memo cites *inter alia* a role for food aid in famine relief, and in the building of national food reserves and stocks (both in the short and medium term), as likely to enhance the development of recipients. Food aid as a means of overcoming a foreign exchange constraint within a recipient country is seen as a longer term benefit and maybe as important as other forms of aid. Disincentive effects at the international level, the Memo claims, can be reduced by observation of the principles of surplus disposal and local disincentive effects can also be overcome by the stipulation that food aid should not be sold in open market sales at below normally prevailing internal prices. Food aid could also reduce inflationary pressure in recipient countries by giving balance of payments relief and improve employment within the recipient country. In this theoretical catalogue of potential benefits, the Commission did not however provide any evidence of its programmes having contributed to recipients economic development, as opposed to general food aid emergency assistance.

The 1974 Commission Memo argued for a more 'purposeful food aid policy' which would comprise of adopting a principle that all future food aid would be in the form of Community actions. The core of this argument rested on the 'coherence, efficacity and close relation between food aid policy of the community and agricultural policies which are of a community character'. The future commercial benefit from (for example) skimmed milk powder would in due time create a commercial demand for dairy plant equipment from the Union, although care was taken in the Memo not to suggest an increase in commercial demand amongst recipients of European milk powder itself.

From 1968 to 1974 EU food aid policy was framed in the thinking that related to the direct linking between agricultural protection and surplus disposal and the channel for EU food aid was predominantly multilateral, namely the WFP. The European Union did not have the operational capacity to establish food aid based on development projects and programmes, and it was therefore pragmatic to channel food aid through the UN system (as well as being less costly). The procurement of EU food aid was predominantly from DG VI, that is the agricultural directorate of the European Commission, thus reinforcing the idea of an administrative connection between food aid and surplus disposal. The events of the early 1970s known as the World Food Crisis, that is to say the dramatic rise in world cereal prices and the fall in world reserve stocks, changes the basis of world food aid policy, including that of the EU itself. During the 1990s the link between food aid policy and surplus disposal became weaker and food aid became a relatively scarcer resource than at any time since the 1950s.

The scarcity of food aid resulted in a changing emphasis on policy from all the major food aid donors, including the EU. Food aid as a scarce resource was no longer available in volumes that had characterised the 1960s and surplus disposal as an issue became less pressing for trade competitors. EU Community food aid increased after 1975 as a result of the first enlargement of the Union, which brought further members into the Union FAC quota, and the EU share of world food aid also increased. During the mid-1970s the Commission published a number of documents and memorandum in relation to food aid policy.

The 1974 memo, as was previously noted, emphasised the Community nature of food aid policy and particularly that it was related to the EEC responsibility for commercial policy. Until 1975 the Council of Ministers had in effect confined Community operations to a small part of the overall European programme and to that of the co-ordination of national policies. The Commission claimed that this restriction resulted in incoherence and an actual lack of co-ordination, not only for food aid policy but also development co-operation and agricultural policy. The Council of Ministers, as the representatives of the member states, are responsible for foreign policy and developmental aspects of food aid and the community was responsible for those commercial policy aspects. The consequence of this separation of authority resulted in a cumbersome and ineffective food aid policy.

The Commission acknowledged that the increase in responsibility for half of European food aid policy was insufficient to co-ordinate overall policy (see *Food Aid from the Community*, 1982). The Council of Ministers in deciding food aid programmes, it was argued by the Commission, was the cause of the cumbersome system where fifteen months delay from the adoption of a programme to the aid being delivered to a recipient, was normal. The Commission also argued that some of the member states took too narrow a view of food aid, as only a humanitarian operation rather than considering it as a resource with a wider economic and political usefulness. In addition to this, the Commission considered that the criteria for the allocation of food aid was unclear, as were the regulations applying to food aid. There was also a lack, or a nearly complete absence, of the monitoring of the effects of food aid in recipient countries. The Commission took the view that, because of a lack of machinery, food aid was not co-ordinated with other forms of development aid and that the use of counterpart funds from the sale of food aid in recipient countries was not property monitored.

The Commission recommended that the community adopted a multi-annual programme, increase the quantity and diversity of food aid products and delegate greater responsibility to the Commission itself. The European Parliament, seeking greater authority in the sphere of development assistance, including the formulation of food aid policy, supported the recommendations of the Commission for a change in policy. The Commission also recommended the developmental objective of agricultural self-sufficiency for developing countries and that European policy should support this objective since it was a primary purpose of the CAP (see Cathie, 1990 and Sturgess, 1995). The Commission also recommended an increase in triangular transactions, which the Council of Ministers endorsed as they did the setting up of buffer stocks in recipient countries.

European Union food aid policy in 1982 emphasised three broad criteria for the allocation of its commodity aid:

- nutritional actions which were determined by a food short-fall in a recipient country;
- the level of economic development as measured by an upper limit on per capita income of $750 (in 1982) as determined by the World Bank;
- and the external financial position (as determined by the IMF) of the balance of payments in absolute terms and the payments ratio.

These criteria introduced economy-wide measures for the general assessment of potential recipients of EU food aid and implies that this form of aid can contribute to the economic and social development of the recipient economy in the longer term. This change of emphasis contrasts with food aid as a short term humanitarian or relief resource, although the Commission had assessed the food aid programme to 1982 as having had little effect as an instrument of development.

The early 1980s also saw the Commission propose a broad food strategy policy for developing countries with an emphasis on food security objectives, and particularly investing Community food aid with a range of resources so that it can help developing countries attain self-sufficiency in food production. The emphasis on a food strategies approach by the Commission, to some degree anticipated the economy-wide emphasis of the Structural Adjustment approach of the World Bank and the Conditionality approach of the International Monetary Fund. The Commission's emphasis on a food strategy approach for developing countries saw the solution to the growing food crisis of the 1980s, particularly in Africa, as not being found through an increase in food supplies via food aid, but an increase in the supply of food within developing country's own production.

During the 1980s European Union policies towards developing countries, both aid and food aid policy, sought to promote supply-side increases in food from developing countries themselves. This strategy saw as policy instruments; the promotion of regional integration of food producers; the promotion of national and regional food policies, such as those in the Southern African Development Coordination Conference (SADCC); and the use of triangular transactions between developing countries, as an instrument of food security and increased trade. Self-sufficiency and national and regional stock policies were also thought to be instruments that would enhance both the supply of food and overall food security, (see Koestler, 1986).

The formulation and management of European food aid policy during the 1970s was determined by a mixture of external and internal events. The change of world market conditions, particularly the rise in cereals prices and the shortage of surplus capacity including food stocks, resulted in a re-assessment of food aid policy amongst the major donors. The EU began to formulate its own policy while still continuing to support the project-based multilateral food aid policy of the UN system. EU policy was developed with the Lome Conventions, beginning in 1975, to consider a broad policy framework with trade and developmental initiatives, that were to be distinctive in their character. Food aid policy, while not exclusively designed for ACP countries, was one of a range of developmental policies that emerged during this period.

EU development policies emphasised the importance of agricultural development in Third World countries and attempted to provide a very general policy framework to promote such development in the Third World. This framework included, *inter alia*, frameworks for regional integration; particular trade and aid agreements with ACP and other

74

developing countries; specific agreements within Lome on agricultural commodities and minerals; and the granting of preferential trade access to the Union. The EU was designing its overall aid and trade policy within the scylla of its international obligations such as the GATT and the FAC, as well as the IMF and the World Bank and the charibydus of the member states' individual aid policies which differed through their own historic experience and their actual and perceived different developmental priorities.

The EU, in designing its own policies in broad thematic frameworks with an emphasis on multilateralism, would avoid conflict and contradiction that would inevitably follow from a direct attempt to reconcile nation developmental policies into a unified European policy towards the Third World. The sum of all the national member states' development and aid policies would not add up into a coherent and consistent overall policy that would be uniquely European. Food aid policy as a subset of European national policies and as a subset of European union aid policies has fundamental differences of objectives that cannot be easily reconciled by a process of fudging. The objective of the promoting of self-sufficiency in agriculture in developing countries using buffer stocks and inevitably the price mechanism, does not reconcile with free trade and free markets in agriculture. As was previously noted in Chapter Three, the French support of the self-sufficiency objective in agriculture and the British/German emphasis on free trade in agriculture sit uneasily together in a common policy framework.

The Commission emphasis and that of the WFP, on triangular transactions may be considered as a means of reconciling free trade and protectionist elements within the broad objective of food security policy. Self-sufficiency and regional trade within regional blocs and groupings is promoted by the EU. The concept of self-sufficiency has had a trade element added for a food security objective, that to some degree may moderate the issue of both the inappropriateness and the high costs of such an agricultural policy framework. The experience with the high costs of the CAP does not suggest that such a food security objective replicated in regions of the developing world would necessarily be the first best option and may not even be the second best option either.

The formulation of EU food aid policy was not only a response to the change in world market conditions, but also part of the wider objective of establishing a distinctive European-wide policy for aid, trade and development. Both the Commission and the European Parliament took the view point that this could only be achieved if the responsibility for the management of food aid policy and operations was to reside with the Commission itself rather than with the Council of Ministers. The food aid policy (and aid policy) of the European Union devised by the Council of Ministers would be the sum of national food aid policies and not a distinctively unified overall European policy. The Council of Ministers would also be subject to compromise and of delay in decision making. The Commission had proposed under the Development Commissioner Pisani in 1983 that the Food Strategies Plan of the Union would provide £31 million to support ACP countries reform their agriculture and encourage self-sufficiency. This proposal resulted in a public wrangle between France and Britain, with the latter refusing to support the policy initiative.

The argument appears to have been centred upon whether the proposal should be exclusively focused upon ACP countries which France considered to contain the world's least developed countries, and Britain who wanted the proposal to include non-ACP countries such as Bangladesh and India. In addition, Britain did not wish the funds originally proposed as £85 million over two years, but insisted that £31 million over eighteen months was sufficient. The disagreement between France and Britain was characterised in the press as one of the two countries pursuing their former colonial interests, rather than being a net addition to a particular European initiative to combat hunger (see *Guardian*, 15th June, 1983).

The Food Strategies programme of the Union to use food aid and financial aid for the reform of agriculture selected four countries in Africa: Mali, Kenya, Rwanda and Zambia (Tanzania had also been selected in 1982 but was subsequently dropped from the country list). Council Regulations 3331/82 had stipulated that food aid should be integrated with other forms of European assistance such as technical and financial aid. These Food Strategy programmes of the Union were not notable for their success, since the four countries concerned have not achieved increases in agricultural output or effectively improved their overall economic situation, since neither the levels of self-sufficiency in each of these countries has improved, nor has the level of nutrition amongst their population.

Twelve years after the Food Strategy initiative the four countries concerned are less food secure than they were in 1982. The European Union food strategy approach in Africa has not proved a success, given that the country models chosen for a variety of reasons have not been able to sustain their agricultural production. In the case of Rwanda, civil war and ethnic tension resulted in the murder and starvation of millions and EU food aid has been provided as emergency and humanitarian aid, rather than developmental aid. In Zambia macro-economic instability and mismanagement of the agricultural sector has resulted in greater imports of food. Kenya has also been unable, as has Mali, of achieving self-sufficiency in agriculture.

The Commission argued in the mid-1980s for the breaking of the link between food aid management and the management of the common agricultural policy. The Council Regulation of 1986 (3972/86) on Food Aid Policy and Management forms the basis of current EU Food Aid Policy and Management (OJ/L 370 of 30th December, 1986).

Food Aid aims:

- to promote food security in the recipient countries and regions;
- to raise the standards of nutrition of the recipient population;
- to help in emergencies;
- to contribute towards balanced economic and social development;
- to support efforts by recipient countries to improve their own food production.

Since 1986 there have been a number of further council resolutions on food aid policy. In 1988 the Council Resolution of 23rd November emphasised that food security in sub-Sahara Africa was a regional priority for food aid supplies. In 1989 the resolution of the 21st November suggested the integration of food aid with structural adjustment support, while Council conclusions on the 25th June 1990 were that food aid should integrate with other forms of development assistance. In 1991 on June 27th Council resolved that there was to be in particular 'an efficient and optimum use of counterpart funds'.

These Resolutions, taken together with regulations and guidelines, suggest a change in emphasis in European policy moving from the supply side food strategy interventions of the early 1980s towards wider objectives of a food security policy that incorporates economy-wide

77

structural adjustment and economic reforms (see E.J. Clay et al, 1994). It remains to be seen whether EU policy on food aid directs its supplies towards the mitigation of the short-run adverse effects of policy reform as is advocated by the WFP and ADB (WFP/ADB,1986).

The emergence of European food aid policy is subject to the broad agreement of the Council of European Development Ministers, whose regulations and resolutions offer broad and general indicators on the direction of food and other aid policies to be pursued by the Union. The generality of this guidance is subject to compromise and it is often of the most bland form of indication. EU policy operates within the framework of international treaties such as the Lome Convention and the Food Aid Convention. Policy is also constrained by agreements reached by the member states of the Union, with the IMF and the World Bank, as well as Agreements made by the Union with the WTO and UN Agencies such as the WFP, the FAO, IFAD (International Fund for Agricultural Development) and the WFC (World Food Council). The provisions in the Maastricht Treaty for a common foreign policy will entail increased co-ordination of national development policies (Article 130X) at both the operational and policy levels, as well as at international fora. Title XVII, 130 U of the EU Treaty also requires that EU and member states development policy will be complementary.

Complementarity may result in a 're-nationalisation' of development co-operation, or greater control of national development programmes by the Commission. This balance has yet to be decided. In the field of food aid policy there is a greater degree of Commission authority for these programmes since the Union is directly involved with international agreements such as the Food Aid Convention, and it is also directly represented on the FAO and WFP where food aid matters are considered as part of the UN system. The Commission has observer status with the World Bank and the IMF, and the national members with direct representation on these bodies; are not enthusiastic over co-ordinating a European development policy perspective (Courier 154, 1995).

The EU countries hold 28% of votes on the Executive Board of the World Bank which is an unco-ordinated position with regard to development co-operation. With the Food and Agricultural Agencies of the UN system, the Commission as a representative of European policy on food aid matters is in a position to formulate policy, albeit within the bland guidelines of the Council of Ministers. It is because the Commission has had direct responsibility in the first instance for negotiating a European position on the FAC of the IWA and of being directly involved with the multilateral food aid system that a European policy in these matters has emerged, gradually eclipsing and absorbing the national members' own food aid policies and the EU single policy is becoming predominant.

European food aid policy is one of the few areas of development co-operation amongst the fifteen member States where a consensus is gradually emerging and a useful overall policy is possible under the direction of the Commission. Lome as a framework for a unified Europe-wide development co-operation policy on economic aid is still subject to national member interests (and their own foreign Policy objectives) and is unlikely to be delegated to the Commission, or the European parliament without considerable controversy and dispute. In addition to the Council of Development Ministers Resolutions and Regulations for food aid policy and management, the Commission has the power to frame general rules and regulations for the mobilisation of food aid in the form of Commission Regulations.

In 1986 and 1987 the Commission re-organised responsibilities amongst the twenty Directorates General, reducing them to eighteen in number however, in the 1990s this number has been increased to twenty four (see Table VI). Prior to this re-organisation in the 1980s, food aid policy and operations were primarily the responsibility of DG VI Agriculture because of the surplus FAC/IWA relationship with the CAP. The national intervention Boards in the grain markets of the EU were the means of procuring surplus agricultural commodities (on competitive tender basis) for DG VI who arranged procurement, transport and supply to recipient countries under the general guidance of the Council of Ministers.

The Council of Ministers have a Food Aid Committee who provide detail on allocations to recipients. The introduction of triangular transactions and 'substitution actions' (substitution of cash for food surpluses) in the early 1980s broke the link, such as it was, for cereals with food aid as surplus disposal and food aid as a wider part of development policy involving a number of aid instruments. This change in policy resulted in a Food Aid Service in DG VIII, the development co-operation arm of the Commission which has responsibility for Lome and

Table VI
Directorates general of the commission

+	DGI	-	External Economic Relations
	DGII	-	Economic and Financial Affairs
	DGIII	-	Industry
	DGIV	-	Competition
	DGV	-	Employment,Industrial Relations and Social Affairs
+	DGVI	-	Agriculture
	DGVII	-	Transport
+	DGVIII	-	Development
	DGIX	-	Personnel and Administration
	DGX	-	Audiovisual, Media, Information, Communication and Culture
	DGXI	-	Environment, Nuclear Safety and Civil Protection
	DGXII	-	Science, Research and Development
	DGXIII	-	Telecommunications, Information Market and Exploitation Research
	DGXIV	-	Fisheries
	DGXV	-	Financial Institutions and Company Law
	DGXVI	-	Regional Policy
	DGXVII	-	Energy
	DGXVIII	-	Credit and Investments
	DGXIX	-	Budgets
	DGXX	-	Financial Control
	DGXXI	-	Customs and Indirect Taxation
	DGXXII	-	Education Training and Youth
	DGXXIII	-	Enterprise Policy, Distributive Trades, Tourism and Co-operatives
	DGXXIV	-	Consumer Policy Service

(Source: EC London Office)

+   DGs with responsibilities for Food Aid and Food Aid Policy.

the ACP countries. The Food Aid Service of DG VIII of course assumed a wider responsibility for developing countries since food aid was not exclusive to Lome partners.

DG I External relations (foreign affairs) has responsibility for Asia, Middle East and Latin America where the EU has particular regional development programmes and agreements. DG VI still retains responsibility for mobilisation, although its policy role has been transferred. However, DG VIII and DG I divide responsibility for food aid policy with regard to food aid for developmental purposes in ACP countries and in Asia, the Middle East and Latin America. In 1991 the European Community Humanitarian Office (ECHO) was established to deal with humanitarian and emergency relief.

In addition to the council of Ministers (who represent national food aid perspectives and policies) and DG I, DG VI and DG VIII of the Commission having responsibilities for food aid policy formulation and practice, two other bodies have an influence on food aid matters. The European parliament comments on the food aid budget and it also influences policy through Resolutions. During the African Food Crisis of the mid-1980s, the parliament was concerned to press the Council of Ministers to take greater actions and pressed for a greater humanitarian use of food surpluses. The European parliament frequently sides with the Commission on food aid matters since it is in the interests of the parliament to require greater accountability from the Council members and from the Commission itself.

The European Court of Auditors is yet another body which, through its reports to the parliament on the operations of EU policies, provides analysis of the results of these policies and programmes and scrutinises the Commission's finances. In 1981, for example, the Court of Auditors' report on the quality of food aid noted that in ninety cases of food aid deliveries the European system had broken down (*Times*, 3rd September, 1987). The Auditors' analysis of twenty-two countries between 1981 and 1985 indicated that poor quality food had been delivered to fourteen countries and this poor quality applied to all the products given as aid. The re-organisation of the responsibilities for food aid policy away from DG VI towards DG VIII and DG 1 was one consequence of the auditors' findings, although the Commission need only take note of the Court of Auditors' reports and not necessarily act upon them. However, to ignore trenchant and substantiated criticism would weaken the Commission's standing and therefore be unwise.

In 1995 the Council of Ministers proposed yet another new regulation on food aid. Its purpose was to bring together all the existing legal instruments on food aid into a single body of rules. In addition to the legislative changes, the new regulation indicates that food aid is a key component in a long-term food security strategy and that the instruments of this policy will be *structural food aid, local purchasing and triangular operations* with the aim of contributing to the development of agriculture, food security and the promotion of local trade and the inter-regional economy in developing countries. The substitution actions within the food aid programme can be used to purchase seeds, fertilisers, tools and other inputs, or to build reserves and conduct public information and training campaigns. The new regulation formally adds Eastern Europe to the list of potential recipients of EU food aid to over 120 countries (Courier No.153, 1995).

The formulation and management of EU food aid policy is a complex political and bureaucratic process involving a wide variety of international, national and European interests and institutions. Policy formulation and the changing policy emphasis of European aid and food aid programmes reflects the multiple nature of these interests and institutions who are involved in the process. Because of this complexity which mixes multilateral objectives and national objectives, a blend of European policy appears to be emerging with the Union moving towards a unified food aid policy and programme.

5 Multilateral food aid policy, non-governmental aid organisations and the food aid policy of the European Union

5.1 The relationship between multilateral food aid policy and European food aid policy

The European Union had been a signatory to the establishment of the World Food Programme and multilateral food aid system of the United Nations in 1963. This programme had been experimental in so far as it adopted a policy of specialising in small project-based food aid allocations to a large number of developing countries. The project approach contrasted with what had been the predominant form of food aid allocations, namely a programme approach of the US PL 480 Programme. Multilateral food aid was to be used, not only for relief and emergency purposes, but also to assist in the social and economic development of recipients (see Cathie, 1982 for a discussion of the policies and programmes of the WFP).

To avoid price displacement effects WFP food aid was given in the form of grants and was not to be sold in recipient markets. After a three-year experimental period with relief and project based food aid allocations, the WFP became a permanent feature of the world food aid system. The WFP receives pledges or donations in cash, or kind from nation states who support the multilateral system. In its early years, during the 1960s, the United States provided over 50% of the resources for the operation of the World Food Programme. When the European Union established its own food aid programme in 1968, it committed

83

some of its cereals food aid to the World Food Programme as part of its obligation to the multilateral food aid system.

In the period from the beginning of the EU food aid programme 1969 until the World Food Crisis of 1974, some 16% of Union cereals food aid went to the multilateral system. The International Red Cross received nearly 8% of EU food aid, the WFP 4%, and the United Nations Relief and Works Agency for Palestine refugees (UNRWA) received some 4% of the cereals food aid. The EU cereals food aid for the period 1969-74 was 1.8 million tonnes of which 84% went to thirteen developing countries on a grant basis as programme food aid.

During the period 1975 to 1980, of the 3.3 million tonnes of Union cereals food aid 26% was given through the multilateral system with the WFP receiving some 11% of this aid. The International Red Cross, the UNHCR (United Nations High Commission for Refugees), UNICEF (United Nations International Children's Emergency Fund) and the UNRWA received 15% of Union cereals aid for disbursement. In the first ten years of its cereals food aid the EU allocated an increasing share of its donations to the multilateral system from 16% in the first half of the period, to some 26% in the second half of the period.

In 1970 the EU introduced two new commodities to its food aid programme skimmed-milk power (SMP) and butteroil. From 1970 to 1974 the WFP received 72% of the SMP for its joint operations with the Union, 'Operation Flood' in India (see Chapter Six for a discussion of 'Operation Flood'). The WFP also was the main channel for some 70% of butteroil during this period. From 1975 until 1980 the EU assumed a greater responsibility for Operation Flood, with some 19% of its SMP going directly to Operation Flood as Union aid and some 28% of its SMP being channelled through the WFP. Butteroil was given to India under Operation Flood in a similar proportion to that of SMP.

The period of the 1970s saw a relative scarcity of cereals for food aid but surplus SMP were available as food aid well in excess of viable projects and programmes (see EEC Community Food Aid 1982). SMP and butteroil are expensive forms of food aid and in value terms during the 1970s and 1980s the Union dairy food aid programme accounted for half of the programme by value but less than 10% by weight (*Real Aid*, 1990).

During the mid-1970s the EU began supplying its food aid, particularly

SMP, to non-governmental aid organisations (NGOs or NGAOs) such as Diakonisches Werk, Cartias Belgica, and Oxfam for use in their own projects and programmes. The EU food aid programme developed a close relationship with international and charitable organisations during the 1970s where it supplied an increasing share of its food aid resources to these organisations. By the 1990s in value terms the EU food aid budget was divided approximately one third bilateral, one third multilateral and one third to NGAOs (Clay et al, 1994).

Multilateral food aid policy and the policies pursued by NGAOs have had a major influence on the shaping of EU food aid policy. This has happened through a direct influence on the food aid policy emphasis of the member states of the Union, on the Commission itself and upon the European Parliament. The multilateral food aid policy of the WFP was developed during the 1960s with a mandate to specialise in project food aid and emergency relief. The WFP had been an off-shoot of the UN Food and Agricultural Organisation and in its early years was influenced by its policy emphasis toward agriculture and agricultural trade. The FAO view of agricultural development was explicitly interventionist, believing that the world food problem would be tackled effectively by direct intervention in national and international markets to achieve social, economic and agricultural goals. The Common Agricultural Policy of the EU in some senses is an example of the dirigiste policies that were advocated by the FAO in the 1950s, where agriculture was seen to require special measures, of both an economic and technical nature, in order to provide sufficient stability that would in turn provide increases in productivity, total output and even maintain employment in that sector.

The experience of the collapse of world markets, particularly commodity markets in the 1920s and 1930s, prompted interventionist mechanisms and arrangements such as monopoly marketing boards, cartels and international commodity agreements throughout most countries in the world economy. This belief in a special position for agriculture and agricultural producers was carried over into the FAO when it was established in the 1940s and the interventionist legacy has characterised the policies advocated by this agency of the UN to the present time. The instability of agricultural commodity markets both in terms of output variations due to weather and other causes, as well as price instability, are seen as a source of disruption that is damaging for producers and for the longer term prospects for sustained output. In the case of both transitory and chronic food insecurity the belief at the FAO is that a number of agricultural instruments of intervention will contribute to increase food security, particularly in poor countries (see Cathie and Dick, 1987).

The stockpiling of staple foodstuffs is considered as a suitable method of overcoming variations in both price and output of agricultural produce. Price stabilisation policies, it was argued, would simultaneously benefit both producers and consumers. In the case of producers the reduction of the range of price variability of agricultural products would provide a means of off-setting uncertainty and, to some degree, risk emanating from particularly world markets. In the case of consumers, price stability would provide supplies at assured prices. The difficulty with this price stabilisation approach is that the requirements of producers and consumers are not easily reconciled since as a rule producers prefer higher prices and consumers prefer lower prices. The intervention agency either at the national or international level requires an ever increasing range of policy instruments: monopoly marketing boards, quotas, direct intervention with the price mechanism and government revenues from the tax system, or aid from donors.

The experience with this form of agricultural policy in sub-sahara Africa has been blamed for the fall in agricultural output during the 1970s and 1980s (World Bank 1986). This FAO approach requires considerable resources, and the cost of such interventions can be both high and ultimately such policy actions can be counterproductive. Stock management at the national and the international levels require substantial resources and informed judgments by managers on stockpiling. The appropriate size of stocks to be held, the stabilisation of prices and output involves complexities and costs that are far from straight forward. Floor-price schemes, price bands and price pegs require considerable sensitivity in their operations that few developing country agencies are able to provide (see Williams and Wright, 1991 for a discussion of the problems and options with storage and commodity markets). More often than not, trade is superior to storage as a means of ensuring food security in the longer term. The misjudged release of food stocks may often as not cause instability in national and international markets, undermining the policies' intended purpose of stability.

The European Union is an advocate of national food stock policies and regional food stock policies as a means to promote food security and agricultural stability in developing countries and its food strategy emphasis of the 1980s, was very much an FAO/WFP policy emphasis. The EU encouraged the formation of the Southern African Development Co-ordination Conference (SADCC) in the 1980s to focus upon a regional stock holding policy for the purposes of increasing food security in the region (see Koestler for a discussion of EU's proposals in the 1980s). The EU was, however, not prepared to underwrite the costs of such a programme.

Allied to policies of intervention in agriculture through stock policies, is the emphasis on achieving self-sufficiency in agricultural supply. Self-sufficiency, as has been discussed, is the centrepiece of the EU CAP. While the Common Agricultural Policy of the EU has been costly to European consumers and taxpayers, and to third parties, the social and political dimensions have been considered as a justification for these policy interventions, particularly by France. The Community food strategy and food aid policy emphasis advocates the principles that underpin the CAP as a suitable model for developing countries in their attempts to promote agricultural growth, prosperity and stability.

Self-sufficiency as a policy objective is not applicable to all countries since it may over-ride the comparative advantage of the economy and result in economy-wide distortion and misallocation of scarce resources. For poor or low income agricultural countries the impact of interventions has not resulted in sustained agricultural development. The FAO/WFP/EU advocacy of interventionist agricultural policies runs counter to the policy proposals and advocacy of the Bretton Woods institutions who consider these as likely to result in the failure of government policy since these policies are financially, and economically, unsustainable as well as being a deadweight on economic growth.

The European Union food strategy and food aid policy proposals for developing countries have drawn from the thinking of the multilateral Food and Agricultural Organisation and the World Food Programme. Food security policy is proposed within a framework where market failure is seen as the central problem, as it is seen to be with the agricultural situation within the EU itself.

The multilateral food, agriculture and food aid system of the United

Nations has spawned Agencies and Committees in each decade since the establishment of the FAO in the 1940s. Many of the Agencies and Committees have overlapping functions and were created as a response to a particular issue, or problem, or a change in emphasis with regard to food and agricultural problems in the world economy. The responsibilities in the UN system and international system for the co-ordination of food aid policies and information-gathering on food aid, is divided wastefully amongst seven international Committees, or Agencies.

The Development Assistance Committee (DAC) of the OECD collated data on food aid until 1989 and responsibility for the monitoring of global food aid flows was assumed by the WFP in its International Food Aid Information System (INTERFAIS). The FAO Committee on Food Security meets annually and is largely confined to being a discussion group. The FAO Committee on Surplus Disposal (CSD) reviews all non-emergency food aid transactions to ensure that export dumping does not violate the principles of surplus disposal. Since the volumes of programme food aid (concessional sales particularly) have reduced, its functions have somewhat diminished from its role in the 1950s and 1960s. The FAO and Global Information and Early Warning System (GIEWS) collates information and reports to donors on the food situation and food aid requests in developing countries.

The Food Aid Convention of the IWA is yet another international body involved in monitoring food aid flows. The World Food Council, established in 1974, meets annually in Rome to consider global food security and the food situation in developing countries. With such a large number of organisations involved with the overseeing of world food, agriculture and related trade and food aid policy issues, it is not surprising that it is difficult to obtain an accurate overview of the food aid and food situation in developing countries. The issue of trade sensitive data and of confidentiality also plays a part in the inevitable incompleteness of data as well as its inaccuracy. There does appear to be a case for streamlining the organisational structures of these bureaucracies and establishing responsibilities for international data gathering and information sharing in fewer organisations. This case is particularly strong if co-ordination and international co-operation amongst donors on food security and food aid matters is to be achieved.

The multilateral food, agricultural and food aid system, unlike the general international aid system, has EU Commission representation as body and this has given the opportunity for a European policy perspective to be established and developed, particularly since 1974. Food aid multilateralism has given the EU the international fora to promote its particular policy and programmes with regard to food security, agricultural development and food aid policy. Both the European Union and the UN food aid system have promoted the idea of a greater co-operation and co-ordination between donors and recipients on aid and food aid policy in order to make the international system of food security more effective.

The EU has adopted in 1990 the Food Aid Charter for the countries of the Sahel, in agreement with the governments of that region. The Charter proposes a framework for regional food security and four areas for co-operation:

- the sharing of information, particularly the evaluation of the economic situation in recipient countries;
- consultation on food aid needs with recipients both on timing and quantities;
- the co-ordination of distribution of food aid involving commercial, co-operative, trading and NGAOs' efforts;
- discussions on cereal balance sheets.

The Food Aid Charter is an attempt to increase the effectiveness of food security initiatives on a regional basis, by improving the consultation and co-ordination of food aid to the region. It is also a framework to try to establish in greater detail the role that food aid may play in enhancing food security in the region. The EU has developed within Africa two areas of regional food strategy, that for the countries of the Sahel and for the countries of SADCC. As with its own food security and agricultural food policy the EU has continued to promote regional integration of food and agricultural system as a means of enhancing food security in the world economy. The EU has had an ally in the multilateral food and agricultural system in so far as the objectives of agricultural and food policy have been essentially the same in both cases.

The WFP specialisation on project-based food aid has been supported by the EU in so far as one third of Community actions (at least in value terms) has been channelled through the UN system. The EU has contributed to the WFP international food reserve for emergencies. One third of EU food aid has been given bilaterally to a relatively small number of countries (see Chapter Six) and one third has been channelled through NGAOs.

5.2 Non-governmental organisations and European food aid

The EU first gave food aid in support of NGOs' projects and activities in the mid-1970s, and established a relationship that has grown over the last twenty years. NGOs or NGDOs or NGAOs in Europe, (non-governmental, development, aid organisations) include a variety of voluntary organisations or solidarity agencies. In France NGOs are referred to as ASIs (International Solidarity Associations). These organisations are usually involved in a single issue campaign and action ranging from environment, local and international; development issues specialising in regions; children; schooling; health and particular crisis situation such as the war in Bosnia. Within Europe the sources of funding for the wide varity of NGOs concerned with emergency, humanitarian aid or development, is considerable. The mix of NGOs own resources/public funds varies widely.

In the 1950s and 1960s there were a few NGOs operating in the developing world. By the 1980s the Commission recorded that there were some 313 NGOs operating in developing countries and by the 1990s the number had reached over 2,000 organisations in Europe alone. According to the OECD, there were 1,600 NGOs in Western countries in 1980; this rose to 2,500 in 1990 and today the figure has passed 3,000 (see Courier No.152, 1995). As 'aid fatigue' has grown, and the aid budgets of many OECD countries have reduced or even fallen, NGOs have increased in number, development activity and as a source of non-governmental funds.

In France and Germany, 15%-20% of NGO finance is provided by the State, whereas in the UK State funds are some 40%, but in Italy and Sweden it can be as high as 80%. NGOs divide into secular and non-secular organisations. In Germany political parties have their own accredited NGOs. NGOs have their origins in the inter-war period, essentially as off-shoots of missionary activities in the colonies, usually providing food or charity to the poor. After the second war, a new generation of NGOs emerged and were concerned with promoting small-scale local development, not just charity. Many of these organisations were secular in their origins.

In the 1980s a new form or emphasis with NGOs appeared, some due to the liberation theology, fashionable at that time, emphasising wider social and political theories as a basis for development and moving away from micro-projects as the basis of their development efforts. NGOs increasingly seek to influence national and international policy with regard to economic, social, environmental and political issues. Some have adopted sophisticated, corporate image-making techniques as part of their campaigning (Greenpeace), or have proselytised for their own brand of development, or seek to persuade a wider public of the harm that they perceive the International Bretton Woods policies do in the Third World (Christian Aid). (See Courier No.152 'On the diversity and role of NGOs'; see also 'The Ethics of Collecting Money', Courier No.152).

NGOs have become a prominent and important feature of development aid based essentially on private charitable initiatives, raising money in developed countries for specific needs and causes in the Third World. The range of causes that NGOs represent is quite broad, some specialising in humanitarian and relief operations, some with children-specific projects and programmes, and some with regional specialisms, and others in specific development projects. NGOs have grown in importance as bilateral development aid has declined in relative terms, and has focused more upon the Bretton Wood Institutions' prescriptions for general policy reform including, Macro-economic Stabilisation programmes and Structural Adjustment. These policies have resulted in financial retrenchment, and the burden of economic and social adjustment has fallen upon the poor and vulnerable in developing countries (see e.g. Mosely, Harringan, Toye 1991: Tarp, 1993).

Some NGOs, most notably the British Oxfam and Save the Children Fund have been operating since the 1940s, and the French Médicins sans Frontiéres (MSF), began its operations in the early 1970s. These NGOs are relatively large professional charitable organisations who fundraise within their own country-base, raising private donations through collections, shops and various fund raising activities in support of their development projects and programmes. In 1991, for example, the MSF had some twenty-nine projects operating in Africa, Asia, Latin America and Europe, spending some 50 million ECU, with a staff of 1,000 doctors, nurses and para-medical staff (Courier No.136, 1992). The two British NGOs, Save the Children Fund and Oxfam, are larger organisations than that of MSF and have twice the annual expenditure on projects and programmes. The British based charity Save the Children received about half of its funding from statutory bodies such as the British Government or the EU. In 1994 Save the Children had an annual turnover of £100 million (ECU 120 million), making it one of the larger established NGOs.

NGOs' activities are generally divided into three areas: (i) campaigning, fund raising and lobbying, together with the (ii) logistics and evaluation of their operations and (iii) the actual operations and projects themselves. NGOs range from highly professional organisations that are of necessity increasingly run as a professionally managed business, requiring managerial skills that often sit uneasily with the amateur hopes and enthusiasms that established their operations in the first instance. The NGOs' capacity to influence public opinion, taken together with the media highlighting, the tragedy of civil war and starvation in many countries, has meant that their views and practical experience has an important influence on shaping public policy towards these issues (see Dreze and Sen, 1990).

NGOs have campaigned on a wide variety of issues relating to development, disaster relief and the environment, and increasing influence and shaped national and international policy towards these issues. Greenpeace as an international environmental NGO campaigning in Europe, has managed to reverse both the policy of a multinational oil company and that of the British government towards the disposal of oil rigs in the North Sea. During the 1980s the environmental lobby pressed the World Bank, with considerable success, to adopt an environmental dimension to their development projects and programmes.

The NGOs, to some degree, have an area of overlap or common interest with that of the UN multilateral organisations such as the WFP and the International Relief organisations of the UN, as well as the Red Cross and Red Crescent international agencies. The international Red Cross and many UN agencies, tend to avoid publicity for their activities, by way of contrast many NGOs court publicity and controversy for the purpose of fund raising. Both, however, have embraced the 'culture of poverty', particularly in publicity images and marketing ploys that become insensitive to human dignity and are cynically promoted as brand images for categories of distress and deprivation.

The NGOs are, to some degree, less encumbered by the political and financial constraints, as well as the bureaucratic inertia that pervades the UN system, particularly those involved with food and agricultural development (see Hancock, 1990). Many NGOs as small voluntary organisations, show remarkable initiative and flexibility in their efforts to provide relief and development projects. In some respects their response to a particular calamity can be more timely than that of the longer established UN agencies, although individually the resource-base of the greater number of NGOs is severely constrained.

Although the proliferation of NGOs and their often amateurish enthusiasm can prove problematic, since their capacity for accountability in their operations and co-operation with each other can be limited. In 1994 for example, in Rwanda, over 130 NGOs were operating in refugee camps in Zaire and another 100 NGOs were trying to establish themselves in these camps. The Director General of Save the Children judged that most of these organisations were seeking a high profile for fund raising rather than contributing to the relief efforts in the camps, and there was little co-ordination of these organisations' efforts (Aaronson, 1995).

As EU food aid, food strategy, food security, policies have evolved towards the developing world, NGOs have come to play a larger role in European policy and programmes. This role has taken the form of providing an effective lobby in Brussels and Strasbourg for European development initiatives and in providing an organisational capacity to carry out relief and development operations. This situation has come about for a number of reasons. In 1951, for example, when the UNHCR was established, it was estimated that there were some 1.5 million refugees in the world; by 1992 this number had risen to over 17 million, and the capacity of the UN system and its agencies to cope financially and logistically with this rising number has been inadequate. The number of civil wars in the world is also increasing in the post cold war period.

NGOs have provided organisational and project capacities for relief and development activities that the official national and international agencies, established for that purpose, have been unable to achieve. Official agencies' priorities are usually established on a bilateral government-to-government basis or on a multilateral agency-to-government basis and are subject to political and other considerations. This feature of the international aid and payments system has increasingly given less consideration to the needs of poor people and small projects and initiatives for the poor to help themselves.

The NGOs have specialised in small projects, often on low budgets, to achieve tangible results in improving the condition of the poor. By way of contrast, bilateral and multilateral aid agencies have preferred financially large programmes and projects that may be beneficial to the recipient economy (and the donors themselves) and not necessarily to poor people within that economy. The WFP has as an exception specialised on a large number of small projects with its food aid policy. Bilateral aid has often been tied to benefitting not only the recipient of the aid, but also the giver of that aid. Food aid where its purpose, as in the case of PL 480 in the 1950s and 1960s, was as much to do with the commercial development of US agricultural trade as it was support for the recipient economies is an example of the aid tying (Cathie, 1989). The British ODA support for the Pergau Dam in Malaysia is a more recent example of the tying of aid to a project, which was designed as much for the benefit of British construction firms and British trade as it was for the Malaysian economy.

NGOs in their single issue and project focus have mobilised public support and private contributions for their activities. Their lobbying parliament, particularly the European parliament for policy action and change during the African Food Crisis of the 1980s, has resulted in a tangible change in emphasis of European aid policies. This change in European development and relief policy can be seen by the establishment of a specific European office to deal with humanitarian aid. ECHO, the European Community Humanitarian Office, established in 1991, is in part a response to the increased public awareness of natural and man-made disasters and the pressure placed upon the EU by the media, NGOs and the parliament, to take greater action. In 1975 Europe provided funding of 5 million ECUs for its humanitarian budget; by 1994 the budget of ECHO was 768 million ECU. Food aid can account for one third to half of this budget, and increasingly the EU finances NGOs with food and cash for their activities. As already has been noted, one third of european food aid is earmarked for international organisations such as the Red Cross and for NGOs.

In 1991, for example, the European Union provided 58% of the budget of Médicins san Frontiéres (Doctors without Frontiers). The MSF budget for 1991 was some 50 million ECUs, and food aid provided a significant part of the EU contribution (Courier No. 136, 1992). Increasingly, relief and development NGOs receive support in cash and kind from the EU, and their annual budgets are being "matched" by the European Union resources. Many of the larger NGOs receive half of their resources from the Union. The NGOs of the 1980s are becoming more dependant upon the Union and governments for their resources, as they become larger and more professionally organised and managed. To some degree NGOs represent the non-commercial privatisation of government aid resources.

The NGOs partnership with the EU may result in the determination of their policies and programmes being subject to a financial dependence and a more formal structure to their organisations and activities. With the increase in financial support from the Union has come the need for greater transparency and accountability with regard to the funds spent. In 1995, for example, the Network on Humanitarian Assistance (NOHA) established a code of practice for disaster relief where accountability features prominently in their ten objectives. The NOHA project supported by ECHO involves some sixty NGOs and five European Universities. It aims to co-ordinate information, and by doing so increase the efficiency of relief and development assistance by the non-governmental sector (Courier No.154 1995).

NGOs are able to operate in states or situations providing emergency relief where it is not always possible for national governments, or the EU to operate. The relief NGOs operate on 'the concept of a duty to intervene', regardless of politics in a particular regional or country situation. MSF, for example, in its relief operations in Somalia, identified a course of action that required them to flood the country with food aid in the full knowledge that the victims of the civil war could only be benefitted if, for every sack of food they were to receive, ten sacks had to be distributed (Luxen, Courier No.136). NGOs such as MSF operating in situations of extreme physical insecurity, such as Somalia (1989), Afganistan (1990), the Balkans (1991) and Liberia (1989), have to fudge the situation with their operations, often 'making a pact with the devil' which it would not be possible for a nation state, or even a UN agency to undertake.

Food aid for relief, emergency and humanitarian operations, requires criteria for its use that differs from that of food aid for developmental purposes. Emergency food aid is a stop-gap measure to overcome a natural, or man-made crisis and attempts to ensure that a population can survive the crisis. When the need for emergency food aid has passed, it is often more difficult for these resources to continue, although there are cases where refugee settlements (such as in Palestine) have received continuous food aid over many decades, pending a political solution to the cause of the refugee problem.

In 1982, the EU contemplated supporting the establishment of a Rwandan colony of over one million people in Tanzania as a means of dealing with the economic situation in that country where agricultural productivity had reached a limit, and particularly the high population growth and the limited capacity of the country to sustain the growth of population (see EU Food Strategies 1981). Food aid was to be used as a means of supporting the colony until such time as economic activity could be established in the settlement. In the event, the Tanzanian government refused to adopt this scheme, and the malthusian spectre of civil war between the Hutus and Tutsis and hunger, decimated the Rwandan population in the 1990s.

The use of food aid as a temporary measure during an emergency situation is often the most effective form of economic aid and support for a country or region. The difficulty with this form of assistance comes after and as the period of emergency has passed, and rehabilitation of the economy becomes a priority. Food aid for emergencies and relief and food aid for developmental, and the budgetary support of governments differ because of the time period involved and the appropriateness of this form of aid for the developmental needs of the recipient. In the case of a civil war, or a major national disaster, technical and financial aid may be of greater importance for the reconstruction of a society than is food aid. Each country situation requires its own assessment as to its reconstruction and development needs. Reconstruction is more likely to be undertaken by support from the Bretton Woods agencies and the major bilateral donors rather than from NGOs who are not equipped financially for such a major task.

During the 1990s NGOs have become the most important partner of the EU Union, followed by the multilateral UN system. In 1993, 44% of all operational funding by the Commission (some 200 million ECUs) was given to NGOs. In addition to this funding, NGOs received a substantial share of food aid under that budget. NGOs' operations provide the Commission with a political constituency within Europe, and a means of a wider support for EU aid and food aid policy towards the developing world. NGOs have an operation capacity for relief and development projects which the Council of Development Ministers and the member states have been reluctant to grant to the Commission itself. NGOs have an influence and a presence, particularly through their development campaigning in the member states, that governments and political parties are more inclined to listen to and act upon than they are to the Commission itself.

The re-organisation of the food aid responsibility between DG I, DG VI and DG VIII and the formation of ECHO is a recognition by the Commission of the growing importance of Humanitarian aid (including food aid) in the post cold war world where increasing strife and civil war is becoming a permanent feature in geo-politics. Food aid in the 1990s has become one means of dealing with humanitarian crisis and NGOs may have become an operational arm of the Commission as their dependence on EU funding increases (see Bossuyt and Devellere, 1995). If EU funding continues for the larger NGOs at the level at which it presently has reached, the Union and the Commission particularly will be in a position in which should it wish, or need to, exert pressure on the NGOs for a 'Common European Policy', its budgetary contribution could prove to be a 'golden-share'. The independence of NGOs may eventually be curbed, by their financial dependence on the EU.

NGOs are, of course, aware of the dangers of financial dependence on national governments and, for that matter, the EU itself. It is probably that some of the longer established NGOs would be able to continue their work without European funding. Indeed, as the NGOs become larger organisations, inevitably they become more company or business-minded, if not bureaucratic. This change may result in their effectiveness and flexibility becoming reduced; however there are signs that this potential problem is being recognised and the larger NGOs are changing their organisational structures. The establishment of recipient country NGOs is almost a form of franchising the organisation' activities in developing countries. Oxfam, for example, has recently campaigned within India for finance from the middle classes for its Indian-based projects and programmes. In a number of developing countries, in addition to the established 'international NGAO' forming local independent branches, there are also an increasing number of locally established NGOs being formed.

While some NGOs are more professional than others, particularly those who have been established for decades and have considerable operational and county knowledge and experience, others are more enthusiastic than experienced. A number of NGOs have had a one-issue existence, while others such as War on Want have fallen foul of the charity law in the United Kingdom by becoming more of a political organisation than a charity. The British concept of a charity is not one that is common throughout Europe, namely tax exemptions are given for charitable activities (widely defined) and organisations in the UK, whereas in Europe in member states such as Germany, political parties receive funds from the state for research and for use in development projects in the Third world.

The NGOs have argued for alternatives to the predominant Bretton Woods orthodoxy, highlighting the misery for the poor and vulnerable groups in developing countries as a consequence of structural adjustment policies and conditionality, particularly where this results in substantial cuts in government programmes such as health, welfare and education. Christian Aid, for example, in 1995 launched a campaign highlighting the adverse effects of World Bank and IMF-sponsored policies on the poor in developing countries, (Madeley et al, 1994).

The NGOs have an operational capacity to run small and medium sized development projects and relief programmes which is not always available, in either multilateral organisations or within bilateral aid agencies and is not (as yet) within the operational capacity of the Commission of the EU. NGOs have a growing experience with food aid for emergency use and a capacity to deal with, and cope with emergency operations. NGO experience with project-based food aid has not, however, been as satisfactory as it has been with emergency food aid. Oxfam's experience in the late 1970s, as is recounted in *Against the grain*, is a catalogue of failures and shortcomings of food aid for projects (Jackson and Eade, 1982). Similarly, the WFP project-based food aid programmes have not notably provided examples of unmitigated success

(Cathie, 1982).

The multilateral food aid policies and programmes have provided, particularly in the early years of the EU food programme, a means to channel European supplies and also, to some degree, the definition of the European policy and operations. During the 1970s and 1980s the EU expanded its food aid programme and began to change its objectives moving to increasingly support NGO operations as a partnership with the Union. Its food aid programme became part of a wider and broader set of developmental objectives including a food strategy approach, structural adjustment approach, and a humanitarian emphasis on its food aid programmes.

6 Recipients of European food aid and its effectiveness as a development resource

European food aid is distributed to developing countries through four distinctive channels. The EU itself donates food aid directly to developing countries supporting projects and programmes, or as they are known as 'normal' food aid donations, and the EU supplies food aid directly for emergency and humanitarian purposes. The second channel for European food aid is the programmes, projects and emergency operations of the fifteen member States of the Union. These national actions (see Table I, Chapter Two) are in addition to their contributions to the community programme. The third channel for the distribution of EU food aid is through the multilateral food aid agency, the WFP and other multilateral UN agencies in support of their operations. Finally, the EU give food aid and financial support to NGAOs for their operations in developing countries.

The evaluation of the effectiveness of the European food aid programmes and donations, is not by virtue of the distribution channels, undertaken by the Union itself. Its three 'partners', the member states, the multilateral UN agencies and the NGAOs have responsibility for the evaluation of food aid programmes and projects undertaken in developing countries and supported by EU food aid and finance. The need for co-ordination amongst the partners and common criteria for the assessment of development projects and programmes as well as humanitarian relief operations, has been a concern of the Commission since at least the mid-1970s and as yet has not been achieved.

However, the recent changes in the organisational structure of responsibility for food aid operations and policy within the Commission itself and the earlier introduction of multi-annual food aid programming, should allow an opportunity for the evaluation of food aid operations which has hitherto not been possible, at least to any degree of depth. The EU food aid programme came under criticism in the later 1980s for the low level of accountability with its food aid operations, both from the Court of Auditors and from academic critics of its policy (Court of Auditors, 1987 and Real Aid, 1990). The dairy programme of the Union came under particular scrutiny and criticism, which will be discussed below (6.2 Operation Flood).

The distribution of European food aid through so many channels make the process of accountability particularly complex and tends to divert the focus of attention on the evaluation of the effectiveness of this aid for the development of recipients. While the co-ordination of the activities and operations of donors would provide the avoidance of a duplication of efforts and a greater degree of clarity as to the purposes for which the aid is intended. The Community has not provided examples of the effectiveness of its food aid programmes in which it is clear where the contribution of this type of aid is evident.

The food strategy emphasis of the 1980s, in which food aid would play a prominent part in the reform of the food and agricultural sectors of four African economies (Rwanda, Mali, Kenya, Zambia) has not been demonstrated (see Chapter Four). This is, of course, not to say that the food aid given to those countries did not provide some benefit, but that the benefit of policy reform that was the intention behind the food strategy approach, was in fact not realised. Whether food aid contributed in some way to the attempted reform, or even impeded it, has not been subject to evaluation, which it should have been.

The Commission no sooner having developed its food strategy approach in the mid-1980s began to move from this approach towards a different focus. The food strategy approach of the 1980s was concerned to improve the agricultural supply response of developing countries, particularly African agricultural production. Food aid was considered to be an appropriate resource for this purpose, taken together with policy reform of the kind that emphasised direct intervention in agriculture at a national and/or regional level. Instruments and objectives of policy, such as self-sufficiency targets, emergency stock holdings and triangular transactions, were the key components of this food security strategy. As was previously discussed, these agricultural objectives were grounded in the philosophy that is central to the Common Agricultural Policy in Europe itself. On the grounds of cost alone this strategy is not appropriate for low income agriculturally-based economies, since it is unlikely that the European Union would provide the financial support necessary to underpin such a strategy.

The Bretton Woods agencies, the IMF and the World Bank, are reluctant to support, financially or otherwise, direct interventions in the food and agricultural systems of developing countries since this runs counter to their market-based approach towards economic development. The multilateral food and agricultural agencies, while supporting interventionist strategies for agricultural development similar to that of the European Union, do not have the financial or food aid resources to accomplish these objectives even if they could be realised in the first place.

The food strategy approach of the EU to agricultural development began to be subtly replaced by an increased emphasis upon food security and structural adjustment, moving the Union more in the direction of the orthodox policy prescriptions of the Bretton Woods institutions. These institutions in their policy approach to advising and financially supporting developing countries, emphasise the importance of free markets, free trade and monetary, fiscal and exchange rate policy of a non-interventionist kind. In the area of agricultural policy the Bretton Wood institutions do not support government interventions in markets for either production or consumption objectives and instruments of policy such as monopoly marketing boards, stock policies or food subsidies to producers or consumers. The Bretton Woods view of agricultural and food policy is framed in the context of a food security policy which considers that it is more likely to be attained if markets are free to operate at their maximum efficiency and free from government interventions. With economic growth, it is believed, will come the reduction of poverty over time. Vulnerable groups in the economy can be selectively targeted by government, with or without the support of aid agencies, to alleviate their plight. Blanket subsidies to producers and consumers results in the misallocation of resources, unsustainable budgetary expenditure and an inflationary and exchange rate policy that can lead to economic stagnation or collapse.

The Bretton Woods institutions favour a policy emphasis of self-reliance, rather than self-sufficiency as a policy objective of agriculture. The increase in agricultural output and productivity in their view is best achieved by markets freely operating both nationally and internationally. The EU views agricultural markets as being inherently unstable, and for the purposes of food security consider that it is necessary for governments to intervene in order that the objectives of price and output stabilisation can be realised. Food security policy in the European Commission view requires an active role for government in agriculture because of the inherent market failures within that sector, particularly when climatic conditions are responsible for the supply situation as a source of price and output instability. The Bretton Woods institutions argue that it is more efficient and more effective if a food security policy involves the government holding financial reserves for food purchases, should they be necessary, rather than stocks of staple foodstuffs.

The EU, in broadening its approach from a food strategy to a structural adjustment framework, has recognised implicitly that food security for developing countries is more likely to be realised if the economic position of the whole economy is considered rather than a narrower sectoral approach as a basis for growth, development and food security.

6.1   The distribution of community food aid amongst developing country recipients

European food aid has been given to a large number of developing countries in relatively small amounts. Recipients of European food aid with a few exceptions, are unlikely to depend on this form of aid as a major development resource, or as a major source of their food supplies. The volumes of food aid given to recipients are small in relation to the food supply and the duration over which food aid is given is not continuous.

The EU criteria for community action falls into four categories:
- basic food needs;
- per capita income and the existence of particularly impoverished groups;
- the balance of payments, and finally

- the economic and social impact and financial cost of the proposed action (see Clay et al 1994).

Of these indicators per capita income and the balance of payments situation are clearer guides than the other two criteria for the selection of countries for programme food aid. A statistical analysis of the relationship between the EU criteria for programme food an allocations was undertaken by Clay et al in 1991. The main finding of this analysis was that the relationship between actual food aid allocations and independent variables which approximated closely the indicators stated by donors was limited. The analysis suggests that allocations were not made on the relatively simple indicators of need such as per capita income, or the balance of payments, or food deficits. Analysis of community action was also undertaken by Herrmann et al in 1990 and concluded that the allocation of community action food aid corresponded to the EU allocation criteria for the years 1983-85 but did not do so in the other years analysed. The year 1983-85 as food crisis years may have been years where the EU in its response to that crisis became closer to its own allocation criteria.

Table VII indicates the recipients of EU community and national actions with cereals food aid for the years 1982, 1985 and 1987, and that the food aid volumes to individual recipients are relatively small. The EU policy of distributing part of its food aid through the WFP, as well as member states also following the same policy, explains the large number of countries receiving some food aid. The WFP has always followed a policy, as a UN agency, of the widest coverage with its multilateral donations of the maximum number of countries eligible to receive food aid, rather than concentrating its food resources in larger projects and programmes. Distributional criteria have taken precedence over efficieny criteria, or the most effective use of food aid as a scarce economic resource.

The ACP countries received some 36% of European food aid in 1982, confirming that food allocations are not related to membership of the Lome Convention. The SADCC (Southern African Development Co-ordinating Conference) countries (see Table VII **) in 1982 received 10% of European food aid, and in 1985 13.4% and in 1987 12.9%, allocations that were part of the EU policy of encouraging a regional stock policy for food security purposes. Former French colonies received some 20% of

Table VII
Recipients** of EU (Community and national) cereals food aid
1982, 1985 and 1987

(thousand tonnes)

	1982	1985	1987		1982	1985	1987
Angola*	35.5	53.1	56.9	Liberia	1.7	-	-
Bangladesh	183.0	191.9	198.4	Madagascar	33.6	35.0	32.6
Benin	5.0	4.0	-	Malawi*	1.7	-	5.0
Bolivia	10.0	10.0	22.0	Mali	41.9	83.9	8.1
Botswana	3.0	7.2	15.8	Mauritania	28.8	55.6	15.1
Burkino Fasso	6.7	29.6	-	Mauritius	3.0	0.9	15.1
Burundi	0.4	2.9	-	Mozambique*	76.7	121.0	141.8
Cape Verde	12.8	40.3	31.5	Nepal	4.8	2.0	9.2
Chad	16.0	80.7	7.3	Nicaragua	22.5	20.2	31.3
Comoros	2.0	0.7	1.3	Niger	5.6	109.4	1.5
Costa Rica	4.0	-	-	Pakistan	45.2	108.7	57.0
Djibouti	5.5	7.5	5.0	Peru	7.0	20.9	26.5
Dominion Republic	2.0	2.0	-	Philippines	1.0	2.5	3.6
Ecuador	4.9	2.1	-	Rwanda	1.0	8.5	-
Egypt	205.4	195.8	312.1	Sao Tome	1.0	4.0	3.3
El Salvador	1.1	11.9	15.9	Senegal	22.2	37.0	4.1
Equatorial Guinea	3.6	3.0	-	Sierra Leone	1.4	2.1	6.1
Ethiopia	152.1	358.7	182.1	Somalia	61.1	105.5	79.7
Gambia	2.6	1.0	-	Sri Landa	55.0	30.0	40.0
Gaza	4.2	1.5	1.1	Sudan	43.2	229.4	111.2
Ghana	22.7	8.1	4.9	Swaziland*	0.6	-	0.5
Guinea	6.5	11.9	5.5	Syria	11.7	14.3	12.8
Guinea bissau	16.2	10.9	6.2	Tanzania*	40.8	53.4	5.0
Guyana	3.0	-	-	Thailand	7.2	3.7	4.7
Haiti	19.4	11.8	11.7	Tonga	0.1	-	-
Honduras	4.0	9.2	2.7	Tunisia	60.1	63.2	35.7
India	0.1	-	0.1	Vietnam	14.8	8.7	18.7
Indonesia	5.1	15.0	19.7	Yemen AR	15.5	8.7	2.5
Jamaica	1.0	3.0	2.0	Yemen PDR	0.3	1.0	4.4
Jordan	17.3	7.0	7.5	Zaire	15.0	6.7	6.8
Kampuchea	12.0	4.0	0.5	Zambia*	1.5	31.0	2.6
Kenya	26.0	83.3	16.7	Zimbabwe*	6.4	59.8	4.7
Lebanon	42.9	9.7	17.5	Miscellaneous	96.5	-	-
Lesotho	6.0	12.0	7.4	**Total**	**1570.9**	**2504.1**	**1857.6**

* SADCC Members.   Countries underlined are ACP Members.
** Countries receiving food aid in 1985 and 1987 also include China, Uganda, Togoland, Central African republic, Iran, Mexico and Morocco.

Source: FAO, *Food Aid in Figures*, (1984, 1986 and 1988).

EEC food aid, with countries such as Chad, Somalia, Mali, Senegal and Djibouti receiving substantial imports for the size of their economies.

Five countries, Egypt, Bangladesh, Mozambique, Tunisia and Mauritania account for 70% of EU total monetised food aid flows in the years 1989-91 (see Clay et al 1994). These countries have been major recipients, in volume terms, of EU food aid for over a decade. However, in per capita terms (kg), that is to say kg per capita in percentage terms, Egypt received (30.6), Bangladesh (11.2), Mozambique (31.6), Tunisia (40.0) and Mauritania (35.1) for the period 1989-91. On a per capita ranking EU programme aid has gone to two countries that are food aid dependant: Cape Verde (158.9), Sao Tome and Principe (97.1). Jordan, Grenada and Dominica are economies that are also food aid dependant, but receive their food imports from the US.

Clearly the Community has chosen to spread its food aid over a large number of countries in the multilateral fashion although a few countries, principally small island economies, have had their food (import) requirements met by EU aid. The irregular and haphazard nature of European supplies, although these have increased over the thirty year period, and the distribution of EU food aid through multilateral channels, accounts for this wide spread of countries receiving relatively small amounts of cereals aid. In opting for a general distribution of its food aid the EU has implicitly opted for distributional objectives taking precedence over efficiency criteria.

The general wide country spread of EU food aid gives the community a presence in over 120 countries and gives the impression of a development policy which covers the greater part of the Third World, although the reality of this broad approach is that the significance of the contribution of the food aid given to the greater number of countries in terms of their economic development is limited, if not insignificant. This is, of course, not to say that small projects aided by food and cash do not benefit individuals and communities, but their ad hoc nature and short-term support may not add much in the medium and longer term. Multilateral food aid and project based food aid has a strong welfare and relief bias and capacity, and in contributing to the benefit of individuals may be of greater significance than the more general programme approach to food aid distribution. The evaluation of emergency and relief food aid requires an assessment of its immediate impact in alleviating a particular problem situation, rather than its longer-term effects.

The question of the evaluation of the longer term effects of food aid upon that small number of countries that have regularly received food aid has yet to be undertaken by the European Union. Those few countries that have received food aid in a continuous fashion, in regular amounts, need to be systematically analysed and assessed for the contribution and impacts of nutritional programmes, macro-economic stabilisation, balance of payments support, food-for-work programmes, stock policy and price stabilisation and regional stock policies. The EU, like the WFP, relies on monitoring its food aid programmes more as an audit of commodity use rather than a more comprehensive economic and social analysis of the effects of the aid on recipients. The evaluation of food aid projects and programmes are often more concerned to demonstrate that there have not been negative price displacement effects at the regional, national and international levels of this aid, rather than identifying what positive effects there have been on the welfare and economic development of the recipient.

Recipients of EU food aid can be divided into a number of categories for the examination of the allocation process. Countries such as Angola, Bangladesh, Ethiopia, Lebanon, Kampuchea, Mozambique, Nicaragua, Rwanda, Somalia, Sudan and Syria are all in politically turbulent and unstable situations; with a combination of war, or civil war, or natural calamity as a consequence of natural disaster or the economy being unable to sustain the population. EU food to these countries is of a relief, short-term emergency type and it is a palliative that is a stop-gap and is unlikely to contribute to the longer-term development of the recipient although it does contribute to the alleviation of suffering. In the case of Bangladesh, the Community has been supplying food aid over a longer period time since the economy has been unable to stabilise its population growth and increase its food supplies, since gaining its independence from Pakistan in 1971.

Both Egypt and Bangladesh are two of the regular recipients of the largest single continuous annual donations from the EU (Thomson, 1983 for an analysis of food aid in Egypt). These countries receive, in the case of Egypt, some 8% of their domestic cereal supply as food aid, with the EU contributing 1% and the US, Austria and Canada the remainder Bangladesh receives 5% of its domestic cereals supply as food aid, with the EU contributing 1% and the US and Australia, Canada the remainder. Both these countries are trade sensitive as far as the United States and Australia are concerned. The United States regards Egypt as an export market for its own wheat flour in addition to its food aid commitments, and is wary of the EU in general and France in particular, taking a greater share of this market with a combination of food aid and commercial sales (see Cathie, 1990). The sensitivities of programme cereals food aid as a source of potential unfair competition between cereals exporters, is evident in the two major beneficiaries of EU donations. However, the greater number of EU food aid recipients receive relatively small and irregular quantities of cereals as to not warrant trade concerns.

6.2 European food aid to central and eastern Europe and the former Soviet Republic

The collapse of the Soviet Union in 1989 saw the emergence of a western economic aid response to the break-up of the Communist empire. The supplying of food aid from both the USA and Europe was a major first provision of western economic assistance for the now emerging transitional economies of the former Soviet Union. The European Union and the United States agreed to jointly supply cereals to the former communist republics on a programme supply basis.

Table VIII shows the European contribution to the CEEC (Central and Eastern EuropeanCountries) and FSR (Former Soviet Republics) over the period 1989-92 and it indicates that the former communist bloc received some 25% of the total cereals aid during the period. During the period 1989-91 the major Eastern European beneficiaries of EU food aid were Poland with 63% and Rumania with 30% of cereals food aid. Albania, Bulgaria and the USSR received 0.2%, 3.6% and 2.8% respectively (Benson and Clay, 1992). Poland and Rumania received over 90% of EU and USA donations of food aid to Eastern Europe. This aid provided both balance of payments support to these countries, as well as helping to mitigate some of the adverse social impacts of policies designed to stabilise the economy in the short run and introduce market orientated economic reforms. The allocation of a quarter of European food aid

Table VIII
EU food aid to developing countries, central and eastern European countries and the former Soviet Republic by category of use 1989-92

(A) National actions & Community Action, including through WFP, thousand tons cereals in grain equivalence

Year of Shipment	Developing Countries Non-Project	Project	Relief	Total Developing	CEEC & FSRs Countries	Total
1989	883	556	762	2,201	287	2,488
1990	687	615	1,056	2,358	1,203	3,561
1991	645	656	1,517	2,818	616	3,434
1992	1,012	673	1,312	2,793	912	3,704
4 Year Average	807	673	2,312	2,793	912	3,704
% of total	21.08	18.2	35.4	75.4	24.6	100.0

(B) EU Community Action

1989	545	262	368	1,175	287	1,462
1990	524	336	618	1,478	1,203	2,681
1991	355	343	1,023	1,721	531	2,252
1992	843	616	1,266	2,725	1,468	4,193

(C) EU Member States' Food Aid Actions

1989	338	294	394	1,026	0	1,026
1990	163	279	438	880	0	880
1991	290	313	494	1,097	85	1,182
1992	169	250	649	1,068	73	1,141

Source: WFP, INTERFAIS, E.J. Clay, et al 1994.

caused concern that developing countries would lose out to the transitional economies in so far as food aid would be diverted from the developing world.

The total European cereals food aid did increase as a response to supplying the transitional economies, and therefore it may be premature to suggest that there will be a reduction of food aid supplies for developing countries. Many of the transitional economies' levels of economic development, as measured in terms of per capita income, are lower than the middle income recipients of EU food aid that are classified as developing countries. In terms of EU general criteria for the allocation of food aid (and that of the WFP) many, of not most, of the transitional economies fall within categories that are in effect developing country. Over the period 1989-92, non-project (i.e. programme, monetised food aid) increased, as did relief supplies. The CEEC and FSR countries received food aid primarily as programme food aid for sales in their respective economies, and thus providing revenues for the general budget and foreign exchange savings.

The EU member states food aid actions (Table VIIIc) continued in developing countries while the increase in community actions during the period were primarily due to the increase in transitional economy food aid programmes. The advent of a food aid need in the transitional economies provided the Commission with the opportunity of expanding its operations and field of influence in this area of aid, since the member states have not become involved directly in supplying food aid of any quantity to these economies. The need to co-ordinate food aid supplies with that of USA supplies, made it essential that the Commission should act as the central European food aid co-ordinating authority. The emergence of the transitional economies and the civil war in Bosnia-Herzogovina has opened a new chapter in European food aid policy in two ways.

The transitional economies, contiguous with the EU, have varying degrees of economic and political need. Firstly, the contiguous transitional economies, Poland, Czech Republic, Belarus, Hungary and the Ukraine, are potentially capable of increasing their agricultural productivity and output given a reasonable period for agricultural reform to have effect. Their economic prosperity and their potential for economic stability and growth will depend on their having access to european markets and trade. These economies are unlikely to benefit from food aid and displacement effects from programme food aid supplies may hamper the prospects of agricultural reform and both productivity and output growth. Secondly, EU food aid policy of a relief and rehabilitation kind, however, is likely to increase in those parts of the Eastern bloc where civil strife and disintegration of societies and economies are an outcome of the re-emergence of nationalisms and ethnicity.

The EU, unlike the USA of America, has never had an explicit foreign and commercial policy objective in its food aid policy and programmes, preferring to frame it food aid policy in terms of humanitarian, relief and project focused operations that were multilateral in character. Co-operation with the US on cereal food aid matters, by coordinating joint activities such as in Egypt, and to some degree in Bangladesh, as well as with the joint supplying of the transitional economies after 1989, has brought back elements of commercial policy and foreign policy, and introduced a new dimension into the European programme for which the Commission has responsibility.

6.3   Operation flood

In volume terms cereals have been the main commodity available as food aid over the last thirty years of EU food aid operations. Almost all recipients of European aid have received cereals as programme food aid, or relief supplies for humanitarian projects and programmes. As was previously noted in Chapter Five, during the 1980s skimmed milk powder (SMP) accounted for half of the value of European food aid but only 10% of the weight. The disposal of SMP and butteroil were directly linked to the protectionist policy of the CAP. The excess capacity of milk production in the Union far outstripped Union and effective world demand. Milk products were not subject to the principles of surplus disposal, since they were designed to meet the problems of cereals as food aid (and commercial dumping) and do not apply to the dairy industry and its international trade.

The dairy surplus problem in the Union was evident from the inception of the CAP in 1962 and by 1970 the costs of the programme were escalating, (milk production was 10% above demand at 1977 prices). Indeed, in spite of dairy food aid as a means of disposing of surplus capacity, the Union was forced in the 1980s to introduce milk quotas in order to reduce the costs of the dairy programme and reduce the surplus stocks of dairy products.

In 1969 the World Food Programme began a dairy development scheme in India with skimmed milk powder and butteroil supplied to it from the newly created European food aid programme. The programme, which was named Operation Flood because the SMP and butteroil would flood the main Indian urban markets, were a dearth and shortage had been the common situation. Operation Flood is portrayed as a dairy development project which has multiple developmental objectives, including developing the dairy industry and increasing the supply of milk in urban areas. Its objectives are characterised as a combination of growth, poverty alleviation and nutritional. SMP is highly suitable for relief and emergency operations and projects and programmes undertaken by NGOs and the WFP, with EU dairy aid, have focused upon nutritional objectives.

Operation Flood was originally a pilot scheme to use SMP and butteroil for a large scale dairy development project in India. The WFP had intended that this operation would be a prototype for dairy development schemes in the Third World and was one of the largest Programmes by value that the multilateral agency had undertaken since its inception in 1963. Operation Flood was conceived by a charismatic Indian entrepreneur, Dr. Kurien, who is in charge of the Indian Dairy Corporation. He has been responsible for the development of a modern efficient dairy industry which is located in the four major urban areas of India.

Operation Flood has run continuously from 1969 until the present and is due to continue, before being phased out towards the end of the decade. The supply of SMP and butteroil are reconstituted into milk and sold through retail outlets. The revenues raised from these sales, counterpart funds, are then used or spent by the Indian Dairy Corporation to support programmes that increase dairy production and develop the milk distribution network. The Indian government had established the National Dairy Development Board (NDDB) in 1964 to provide technical assistance to the dairy industry and the provision of EU aid in the form of SMP and butteroil provided, through counterpart funding, resources for the programme's development. The original intention of the NDDB had been to replicate the so-called Anand pattern of co-operative organisation of dairy producers throughout India, using technical assistance to obtain the objective of greater output and broad social objectives for the producers and their families.

Operation Flood has run under three stages: from 1970-78, Flood I; from 1978-87, Flood II; and from 1989-94, Flood III. The EU has, since 1970, given a total of 441,000 tons of SMP and 151,700 tons of butteroil. Valued at 1990 prices this is the equivalent of some 750 million ECUs for dairy development in India. The size of the EU donations makes India by far the largest recipient of EU food aid and Operation Flood the world's largest single dairy development programme and, by implication, the EU's largest development project (Terhal and Doornbos, 1983).

The EU saw the main objective of Operation Flood as the improvement 'of the living conditions of 10 million families of milk producers, the establishment of a distribution network extending over 142 large towns with a total population of 150 million and the setting up of the infrastructure required for India's dairy industry' (*Food Aid from the Community: a new approach*, 1982). The Commission observed that Operation Flood illustrated the potential of food aid policy making a direct contribution to the rural development of India and goes beyond the short-term solution of meeting the country's immediate food requirements.

Ironically, India faces with the EU the problem of an excess of milch cows: although India had some 18% of the world's cattle in 1977, it only had 1½% of the world's output of milk and beef (Crotty, 1977). Critics of Operation Flood argued that EU SMP aggravated the problem in India's dairy industry because it was argued only the wealthy could afford milk, and the prices received for the reconstituted SMP supplement were high and part of the revenues from these were used to subsidise producers who in turn increased the dairy herd. The increase of the dairy herd had a high opportunity cost for alternative forms of agricultural production, and this in turn offset much of the beneficial price effect particularly to the poor producers, thus undermining the distributional benefits of the programme.

Operation Flood II and Flood III were supported by a World Bank IDA loan to half the value of the EU's SMP and butteroil donations, and these programmes contained elements of private sector development, namely that of the co-operative producers' income enhancement, as well as the development of the private dairy sector. Critics of Operation Flood argued in the late 1980s that the dairy aid element of the EU food aid programme was too costly and that the food aid budget could purchase more cereals as food aid and help a greater number of people in the Third World (*Real Aid*, 1990). However, the support of the World Bank for Flood III and both the Commission and the Indian government saw the programme continue.

The cost of dairy aid was a major issue during the 1980s since it was considered to be a very costly form of food aid (Clay, 1983 and Jackson, 1983). This cost issue, rekindled a long-standing question as to what is the appropriate value of food aid (which had originally been raised by Schultz in the 1960s), since the value of this aid to the recipient was considerably lower than the value attached to it by the donor.

Critics of Operation Flood argue that this dairy programme has not achieved its objectives and that it is a convenient way for the EU to dump its surplus milk powder and butteroil. In the 1970s, when the EU sold surplus butter to Eastern Europe, public opinion did not approve. This has not been the case with Operation flood (*Financial Times*, 1987). The EU acknowledged, as did the World Bank, that there were dangers of price displacement effects and greater monitoring of Operation Flood III was undertaken. Critics also argued that the counterpart fund resources were being spent on technical equipment to build a sophisticated network and not on the dairy development of the rural poor, as was the intention of the programme.

Critics have generally argued that Operation Flood has had an urban bias in benefitting the urban rich consumers over the rural poor producers. The EU has, in part, acknowledged some of these criticism by introducing a price formula as part of the monitoring of Flood III, which is designed to ensure that 86% of counterpart funds are spent on village co-operatives, that consumer subsidies cease and that 14% of counterpart funds are spent on processing,.

It is not clear how far the EU Operation Flood to India has contributed to the dairy development of the rural milk producers of India, rather than for the development of an urban industry with considerable technical sophistication, although European dairy machinery interests have benefitted in supplying equipment for the urban milk marketing network.

Operation Flood is a major example of export dumping of surplus agricultural capacity, and its benefits to parts of the dairy industry in India appear to be considerable, but its original intended beneficiaries have not been demonstrated in the considered analysis that has been undertaken (European Court of Auditors, 1987 as well as Doornbos et al, 1991). Operation Flood may have set out to benefit the producers and the rural poor in India, but in the period of twenty-five years of dairy aid supplies, at the least the claim is not proven and at best the urban middle classes and the technical capacity of the dairy industry has received a windfall from the EU taxpayers and consumers.

6.4   Counterpart funds

The issue of counterpart funds as a means of financing real development, both products and programmes, has been a concern with food aid policy since the US PL 480 programme of the 1950s. The US experience with their Title I PL 480 programme food aid counterpart funds was not a happy one. The proceeds from the sales of food aid within the markets of recipients were deposited usually in the central bank of the recipient, and potentially could be used for development projects or programmes. PL 480 Title I food aid programmes, during the 1950s and 1960s, saw counterpart funds grow to the point that in the early 1960s $3.5 billion had accumulated and were unlikely to be spent. Sixty per cent of these local currency proceeds were held in eleven countries: Greece, India, Indonesia, Israel, Turkey, Pakistan, Spain, Taiwan, Vietnam, Burma and Yugoslavia. In the case of Israel, Taiwan and Yugoslavia, they amounted to some 10% of the respective country GNP.

Three issues with respect to the use of these local currency proceeds or counterpart funds emerged. The first was the sheer size and impossibility of spending them, while the second issue related to the donor, the US, attempting to determine their use and therefore being accused of unduly interfering with the developmental (and political) priorities of the recipient. This second issue caused considerable conflict between the US and India during the 1960s, and resulted in a withdrawal of the PL 480 from that country (see Cathie, 1989). The third issue was of a theoretical kind, namely to what extent were counterpart funds real resources since the food aid has been consumed and the funds accumulated from these sales were merely an accounting device. Dandekar (1965) argued that these funds could become a 'fiscal drug' for the recipient government and that food aid would be desired by government because of the revenues produced rather than for the intrinsic value of the aid itself. He suggested that the funds should be earmarked for particular purposes, such as price policy for agriculture on the recipient market economy rather than general budgetary use.

An alternative view of the role of counterpart funds suggests that the impact of these funds are neutral if used to finance productive investment. Srivastava (1972), in his analysis of the impact of PL 480 counterpart funds on India's money supply, viewed this as neutral. Charkravarty and Rosenstein-Rodan (1965) view these funds as nothing but 'shadows', and Shonfield (1965) thought that the counterpart funds of the German Marshall Plan were 'nothing but formalised nonsense'.

In fact the EU Operation Flood policy of the period 1969-2000 has earmarked the counterpart funds produced from SMP sales in India for the development of the dairy sector, although as we have seen the intended beneficiaries of these proceeds have not turned out to be as was anticipated by the Commission. The urban industrial sector and the middle classes have benefitted rather than rural producers of milk and the poor. Operation Flood counterpart funds have, in the main, been spent on the urban milk infrastructure which has been a decision made by the Indian authorities, whereby they have judged priorities in a fashion that has differed from the intended purpose of the original programme. The EU Commission has found that the use of counterpart funds are unlikely to be determined by the donor in India, as the Americans found two decades earlier. The Indian head of Operation Flood, Dr. Kurien, has stated the position with regard to the priorities of the programme, that his judgement "won't be subordinated to anyone, including the EU" (*Financial Times*, November, 1987).

Operation Flood is the largest project within the EU food aid programme where counterpart funds play a prominent role, and these funds are used to finance the development of the dairy industry, as a budgetary contribution to that industry. EU counterpart funds, given the wide country distribution of its food aid and the relatively irregular supply to most recipients, does not pose a particular problem. However, the major recipients of EU programme food aid: Egypt, Bangladesh, Mozambique, Tunisia, Mauritania, are countries where counterpart funds have a potential effect upon the recipient government budget and, for that matter, the balance of payments. In Mozambique, counterpart funds from the sale of cereal food aid provided 22% of government revenue in 1989, and a similar situation also applied to Bangladesh during the early years of its independence (Riley and McLelland, 1990). As the EU moves its food aid objectives in the direction of structural adjustment lending, then it is likely that counterpart funds would be considered as part of the overall government budgetary position in line with World Bank, and particularly IMF orthodox fiscal requirements.

The EU has not had the level of counterpart funds as an adjunct of its food aid programmes, as was the case with PL 480 from 1954 until 1971. The budgetary effects of EU food aid counterpart funds may have some significance with regard to recipients within two groups of developing countries. The first group would include the major recipients as mentioned above, and the second group would be those small food aid import-dependant economies as discussed earlier, namely Cape Verde, Sao Tome and Principe. In these countries, the level of EU food aid imports as such are so high that its budgetary and exchange rate effect is a major determinant on the level of economic activity. Both these small economies would warrant further study on the impact of food aid on their development since they are a clear case of food aid dependence and a policy should be formulated to wean them from this dependence.

The value of EU food aid for the development and growth of recipient economies has not been established by the Commission and there are no studies, even arising from the European food strategies initiative of the 1980s with regard to the four countries chosen for the exercise. European food aid is supposed to be valued at world prices, but a survey undertaken by Maxwell and Owens in 1991 found that of the sixteen countries receiving monetised programme food supplies, seven valued this aid at the domestic market price and nine used the world price. Operation flood values EU SMP powder at domestic prices, rather than the actual cost of the SMP to Europe. The value of the SMP to India is clearly not the cost of producing the surplus in Europe itself. The issue of the value of food aid commodities, particularly cereals and skimmed milk powder and butteroil produced in Europe, to developing countries is as much in doubt as it was thirty years ago. Schultz assessed the value of PL 480 to recipients in 1965 at about one half of the costs of acquiring the original surpluses, to the United States. The value of European food aid to recipients is probably of a similar magnitude to that of PL 480 for cereals and may be considerably less for dairy products.

European cereals food aid, as part of overall world food aid supplies, has been given during a period when the relative supply of surplus commodities have been scarcer than in the period prior to 1974. This relative scarcity of world food aid supplies make it an imperative that these resources are used to their most efficient and effective ends, whether they are given for the purposes of relief, emergencies, rehabilitation or as a contribution to the development of the recipients. The record of European food aid over nearly thirty years does not establish the case for food aid having been a more effective form of development aid over united financial aid. The supplying of food, medicines and other materials for the relief of distressed populations, whether they arise from excess surplus capacity or not, may be the more appropriate use for food aid than as a macro-economic input for the economic development of recipients.

Conclusions

European Union food aid policy has evolved from a narrowly conceived response to agricultural protection which had caused unwanted surplus agricultural products to be given as aid to developing countries. Europe became involved with food aid first as a receiver of that aid during, and immediately after, the second world war, and secondly as a contributor to multilateral food aid in the early 1960s. A European food aid programme was first established in the late 1960s as a response to a request from the United States for a contribution towards sharing the burden of costs and responsibilities of world food aid donations.

Union food aid policy and Union programme was determined in the light of the prevailing multilateral food aid policy that had emerged during the period prior to the establishment of Europe's own programme. From 1968 until the world food crisis of 1974, Union policy was multilateral in its character although this policy had been constrained by concerns with food aid disrupting national and international agricultural markets. The concern with food aid and the surplus disposal of agricultural commodities, particularly cereals, has played a prominent role in providing constraints upon the use of food aid for economic development in the world economy. Food aid has both the capacity to benefit and to harm recipients, it also has the potential to harm third party food competitors of donors. The period of the 1970s and the relative shortage of agricultural commodities, compared with earlier decades, for food aid programmes has meant that the concern with the trade

119

consequences of this form of aid are less acute than they were when the European programme was first established. Trade concerns still cast a shadow over food aid programmes and policy of all the major donors, including that of the European Union.

The Union has explicitly adopted a positive trade emphasis to its food aid and food strategy policy towards developing countries by championing triangular transactions and providing financial support to developing countries for the purchase of food supplies from other developing countries. European food aid policy is still, however, dependent upon its own markets and its home production for the greater supply of its food aid resources. In the two major commodities supplied as food aid, cereals and skimmed milk powder, the relationship between the surplus capacity in the Union, and the availability of these commodities as aid, indicated that SMP is very much a throw back to the consequences of the Common Agricultural Policy. The cereals food aid programme has, in Union policy, broken the link with agricultural protectionism, although both France and Italy in their national food aid programmes retain more than a residual link with their own agricultural capacity.

The EU has embraced the food aid policy of the multilateral institutions of the Rome agencies and particularly those of the WFP and has supplied the UN relief agencies. Europe has also kept within international agreements with regard to the development of her own programmes and policies. While the Union is now responsible for over half of all European food aid donations, national food aid programmes and policies sit beside those of the overall Union. European food aid policy is at present a mixture of fourteen national programmes and one overall Union programme, with the Union having gradually gained more authority in the determination of policy, supplies and resources for its projects and programmes.

The advent of majority voting as a possible outcome of the Maastricht negotiations will result in a tendency for a single Union policy becoming the norm and national food aid policies and programmes reducing as a share of overall European supplies. This outcome is likely because of the desire of the Commission and the European parliament to have a greater role in determining overall policy. While in some respects food aid is a controversial form of development assistance, in other respects it is less controversial for the Commission to dispense this form of aid than it would be with regard to untied financial aid.

The European food aid response to Eastern Europe since 1989 has only involved Union contributions, and these have been administered by the Commission. The attitudes of the Member States towards food is discernable in the overall Union policy, although as policy changes in response to world events a single Union view is emerging. The collapse of the Soviet Union and earlier international crises of 1974 and 1986 have added an impetus to the emergence of a single policy.

Union policy in its allocations of food aid divides almost equally between contributions to the UN multilateral system, its own so called 'normal' programmes and to the support of the operations of NGOs. This division is in part explained by the reluctance of the Council of Ministers to grant a greater operational capacity to the Commission and therefore both the multilateral system and NGOs can meet this requirement from their own resources. Both the UN multilateral system and the NGOs provide additionally a legitimacy to the Union that would have been unlikely to have been granted by the Council of Development Ministers. The multilateral system and particularly the NGOs provide a "development constituency" within Europe that transcends National sectional interests and even National political parties, benefitting the Union, and particularly the Commission, with their support.

The issue of the effectiveness of European food aid as a development resource that is more appropriate for the development needs of recipients, is not at all clearly demonstrated by the results of its programmes over the past twenty five years. The Union has given its food aid to over 120 countries, often in small and discontinuous amounts, with a few countries who have become food aid dependencies and have poor prospects of breaking that dependency. Increasingly, food aid resources are forming a small part of a broader Food Strategy Programme towards developing countries, and in some cases providing balance of payments and budgetary support for wider economic reforms in the form of structural adjustment programmes and policies.

The European food aid programme has also moved, by virtue of the resources it commits towards recipients of its aid, more towards food as a humanitarian resource rather than as a development resource. The EU food aid programme is not primarily a means for the justification of the CAP, but more of a justification for a single European food aid and humanitarian policy. In so far as the programme's emphasis moves in this direction and the Union allows, in due course, access to its markets for developing countries, including transitional economies, it is likely to prove more beneficial to both parties.

Bibliography

Aaronson, M. (1995) "Interview with the Director General of Save the Children", *Courier* No. 152, Brussels.

Adams, D.W. (1968) "Marshall Aid: rebuilding Europe". *History of the 20th century*, Parnell, London.

Agra-Europe (1984) (a) "EEC to allow substitution of financial aid for food aid", June 8.

Agra-Europe (1984) (b) "The EEC's role in international food aid" Agra-Europe Special Report no. 20, Tunbridge Wells.

Agra-Europe (1987) "Community modernises its food aid programme" April 16.

Bairoch, H.P. (1975) *The Economic Development of the Third World since 1900*, Methuen, London.

Bard, R.L. (1972) *Food Aid and International Agricultural Trade, a study in legal and administrative control*, D.C. Heath, Lexington, Mass.

Benson, C. and Clay, E.J. (1992) *Eastern Europe and the former Soviet Union: Economic Change, Social Welfare and Aid,* Overseas Development Institute, London.

Bhagwati, J. (1988) *Protectionism*. MIT Press, Cambridge.

Bos, A.K. (1978) *Food aid by the European communities: policy and practice*. ODI Review No.1.

Bossuyt, J. and Devellere (1955) "The Financing dilemma of NGOs", *Courier* 152, August.

Boyd-Orr, J.B. (1966) *As I recall*, Macgibbon and Kee, London.

Cathie, J. (1982) *The Political Economy of Food Aid*, Gower/St. Martins.

Cathie, J. (1982) *The Development of International Food Aid Policy*, Intereconomics.

Cathie, J. (1985) (a) *Food aid policy and world agricultural trade.* Occasional Papers Series, Agricultural Economics Unit, Department of Land Economy, University of Cambridge.

Cathie, J. (1985) (b) *US and EEC agricultural trade policies: a long run view of the present conflict.* Food Policy Volume 10.

Cathie, J. and Dick H. (1987) *Food security and macroeconomic stabilisation: a case study of Botswana 1965-1984.* J.C.B. Mohr (Paul Siebeck) Tübingen and Westview Press, U.S.A.

Cathie, J. (1988) *Pricing policy and stabilisation: results from Botswana:* paper presented at the agricultural Economics Society Symposium on structural adjustment and food policy in developing countries, Manchester, April.

Cathie, J. and Herrmann, R. (1988) *The Southern African Customs Union, Cereal Price Policy in South Africa and Food Security in Botswana,* Journal of Development Studies, 24.

Cathie, J. (1989) *Food aid and the industrialisation of South Korea.* Gower Press, UK and USA.

Cathie, J. (1989) *Modelling the role of food imports, food aid and food security in Africa: the case of Botswana.* Paper presented at EADI Seminar on assessing the economic impact of food aid. Oslo, February.

Cathie, J. (1990) European Food Aid Policy, *A Review and Assessment 1968-1988.* Paper presented to the Agricultural Economics Society Annual Conference, Wye College, University of London.

Cathie, J. (1993) *European Food Aid Policy 1968-1988*, in Ruttan.

Cathie, J. (1993) *Food Aid and Industrialisation in Korea,* in Ruttan.

Charkravarty, S. and Rosenstein-Rodan, P.N. (1965) *The linking of Food Aid with other Aid.* WFP study no.3, Rome

Clay, E.J. (1983) *Is European Community food aid reformable?* Food Policy, August.

Clay, E.J. and Mitchell, M. (1983) *Is European Community food aid in dairy products cost effective?* European Journal of Agricultural Economics.

Clay, E.J. and Benson M.S. (1989) *Triangular transactions, local purchases and swap arrangements in food aid: a provisional review with special reference to Sub-Saharan Africa.* EADI Working Group on Aid Policy and Performance, Oslo, February.

Clay, E.J. and Benson M.S. (1993) *Food Aid Programmes of the European Community and its member States: a comparative statistical Analysis.* ODI Working Paper 72, London, Overseas Development Institute.

Clay, E.J. and Singer, H.W. (1983) *Food as Aid: food for thought.* Institute for Development Studies Bulletin, vol. 14, no.2.

Clay, E.J. and Singer, H.W. (1985) *Food Aid and Development: Issues and Evidence,* WFP Occasional Paper No. 3, Rome.

Clay, E.J. and Stokke, O. (eds) (1991) *Food Aid Reconsidered: Assessing the impact on Third World countries,* London, Frank Cass.

Clay, E.J. and Singer, H.W. (1992) *Food aid and development, the impact and effectiveness of bilateral PL 480 Title 1 type assistance USAID.* Program Evaluation Discussion Paper No. 15, Washington.

Clay, E.J., Benson, C. and Dhiri, S. (1994) *Evaluation of European Union Programme Food Aid: Stage one.* Overseas Development Institute, London.

Courier (1984) *Special edition on food strategy,* Brussels.

Courier (1988) *Special edition on structural adjustment,* Brussels.

Courier (1989) *Special edition on food aid,* December, No.118, Brussels.

Courier (1990) *Lome IV Convention,* no.120, Brussels.

Courier (1992) *Special edition on Humanitarian Aid,* no.136, Brussels.

Courier (1995) *Special Edition on NGOs,* no.152, Brussels.

Courier (1995) No. 153, Brussels

Courier (1995) No. 154, Brussels

Courier (1995) No. 155, Brussels

Crotty, R. (1977) *"How Europe's milk is becoming India's poison".* Times, 6.5.77.

Dandekar, V.M. (1965) *The Demand for food and conditions governing Food Aid during development.* WFP Study No. 1, FAO Rome.

Delorme, H., Chabert, J.P. and Egg, J (1979) *Food aid policy counter-report: European Community food aid policy, in The European Alternatives: an enquiry into the policies of the European Community,* ed. G. Ionescu. Sijthoff and Noordhoff, Rijn.

Doornbos, M. and Gertsch, L. (1989) *Extending milk routes: internal and external linkages of India's dairy economy.* EADI Working Group on

Aid Policy and Performance, Oslo, February.

Doornbos, M., Gertsch L. adn Terhal, P. (1991) *Dairy Aid and Development: Current trends and long term implications of the Indian case* in Clay and Stokke.

Doornbos, M. and Terhal, P. (1989) *Dairy aid and development: some reflections on Operation Flood.* Working Group on Aid Policy and Performance, Oslo, February.

Dreze, J. and Sen, A.K. (1990) *The Political Economy of Hunger,* Clarendon Press, Oxford, vols. I, II, and III.

Economist (1985) "How much can food aid help the starving?" July 20.

Economist (1995) "The Lome Agreement", November, London.

EEC (1963) L"Aide alimentaire de la CEE aux pays en voie de développement Serie agriculture, 14, Brussels.

EEC (1974) *Evolution of food aid.* Information Directorate-Generale, Brussels.

EEC (1974) *World Food Conference.* Information Directorate-Generale, Rome.

EEC (1982) *Community food aid.* November. ISBN 92-825-2707. Brussels.

EEC (Background Report) (1977) *Co-operation on development.* ISEC/B50/82, London.

EEC (Background Report) (1978) *Community food aid record.* ISEC/B70/78, London.

EEC (Background Report) (1978) *Operation Flood.* ISEC/B39/78, London.

EEC (Background Report) (1979) *Community food aid record.* ISEC/B18/79, London.

EEC (Background Report) (1980) *A new approach to food aid.* ISEC/B44/80, London.

EEC (Background Report) (1981) *A strategy to combat hunger.* ISEC/B41/81, London.

EEC (Background Report) (1981) *Food Aid.* ISEC/B11/81, London.

EEC (Background Report) (1982) *Notes on community food aid.* ISEC/B34/82, London.

EEC (Background Report) (1987) *Strategies against hunger.* ISEC/B10/87, London.

EEC Council Resolution (1978) *Procedures for the Management of Food*

Aid, November 14, 1308/78 (Ass 857). Brussels.

European Court of Auditors (1980) "*Special report on Community food aid*" Brussels: October.

European Court of Auditors (1987) "Special Report No. 1/87 on the Quality of Food Aid the Extent to which Food Aid Products Comply with the Applicable Rules as Regards Quality, Quantity, Packaging, Time and Place Together with the Commission's Replies". OJ/C219/30. Brussels: August.

European Court of Auditors (1988) Special Report No. 6/87 on Food Aid Supplied to India between 1978-1985 (Operation Flood II), OJ/C31, February.

European Court of Auditors (1993) "Annual Report Concerning the Financial Year 1992 Accompanied by the Replies of the Institutions" OJ/C309/36. Brussels: December.

Ezekial, M. (1958) *Apparent Results in Using surplus Food for Financing Economic Development*, Journal of Farm Economics, volume 40.

Ezekial, M. (1958) *Uses of Agricultural Surpluses to Finance Economic Development in Underdeveloped Countries*, FAO pilot study in India, Rome.

Faber, G. (1982) *The European community and development co-operation*. Van Gorcum, Assen. The Netherlands.

FAO (1954) *Disposal of Agricultural Surpluses*, Commodity-Policy Studies 5, Rome.

FAO (1972) *Principles of Surplus Disposal and Consultative Obligations of member Nations*, Rome.

FAO (1980) *Principles of Surplus Disposal*, Rome.

FAO (1984, onwards) *Food aid in figures*, Rome.

Financial Times (1987) "Anti food aid lobby defeated over Indian dairy project", 27thNovember, London.

Foreign Agriculture (1980) *Food Aid Convention*. December. Washington.

Franco, M. (1988) F*ood security and adjustment, the EC contribution*. Food Policy, February.

Fryer, J. (1980) *Food for Thought: the use and abuse of Food Aid in the fight against world hunger*, World Council of Churches, Geneva.

Grilli, E.R. (1993) *The European Community and the Developing Countries*, Cambridge University Press.

Guardian (1983) "EEC Food Aid Fiasco", 15 June.

Hancock, G. (1990) *The Lords of Poverty*, Heinemann.

Hazlewood, A. (1967) *African integration and disintegration*. Oxford University Press, for the Royal Institute for International Affairs.

Henze, A., Dirk, A. and Schneider, B. (1982) *Food aid of the EC and the Federal Republic of Germany to developing countries*. Quarterly Journal of International Agriculture, Volume 21, No.4.

Helldorf, K. von, Bossard, Ch., Hoquet, P. and Szarf, A. (1979) *Food aid policy report, food aid from the European in The European Alternatives: an enquiry into the policies of the European Community*, ed. G. Ionescu. Sijthoff and Noordhoff, Rijn.

Herrmann, R., Prinz, C. and Schenck, P. (1990) *How Food Aid affects Food Trade and how Food Trade matters to the international allocation of Food Aid*, Discussion Papers in Agricultural Economics, no.6, University of Giessen.

Hogan, M.J. (1987) *The Marshall Plan 1947-1952*, Cambridge University Press.

Hopkins, R.F. (1983) *Food aid and development: the evolution of the Food Aid Régime*. WFP/Govt. of The Netherlands Report on Food Aid Seminar.

Huddleston, B. (1984) *Closing the Cereals Gap with Trade and Food Aid*, Research Report no. 43, Washington DC, IFPRI.

Independent Group on British Aid (IGBA) (1990) *Real Aid: What Can Europe Do?* London.

Ionescu, G. (ed) (1979) *The European Alternatives: and enquiry into the Policies of the European Community*. Sijthoff and Noordhoff, Rijn.

Isenman, P.J. and Singer, H.W. (1976) *Food Aid: Disincentive Effects and their policy implications*. IDS No.116, University of Sussex.

Jackson, T. (1983) *A triumph of hope over experience: an assessment of the recent evaluation of the EEC Food Aid Programme* in Clay and Singer, IDS Bulletin, 1983.

Jackson, T. and Eade, D. (1982) *Against the Grain, the dilemma of project food aid*, Oxfam.

Johnson, H.G. (1968) *An economic theory of protectionism: tariff bargaining and the formation of Customs unions*. The Journal of Political Economy, Volume 73.

Jones, D. (1976) *Food and Interdependence: the effects of Food and*

Agricultural Policies of Developed Countries on the Food Problems of the Developing Countries, London, Overseas Development Institute.

Koester, U. (1986) *Regional co-operation to improve food security in Southern and Eastern African countries.* International Food Policy Research Institute. Research Report 53, Washington.

Krostitz, W. (1970) "Milk and Milk Products as Food Aid", Ceres.

Lipton, M. and Heald, C. (1984) *The EC and African food strategies.* CEPS Working Document No.12, Brussels.

Mackenzie, L.D.M. (1979) *Food aid and agricultural markets: considerations in EEC policy,* in Tracy and Hodoc, op. cit.

Madeley, J., Sullivan, D. and Woodroffe (1994) *Who runs the World,* Christian Aid, London.

Marjolin, R. (1989) *Memoirs, 1911-1988.* Wiedenfeld & Nicholson.

Maxwell, S.J. (1984) *An evaluation of the EEC food aid programme.* University of Sussex, Institute of Development.

Maxwell, S. (1987) *EEC Food Aid,* CAP Briefing, London.

Maxwell, S. (1991) *"The Disincentive effect of Food Aid: a Pragmatic approach"* in Clay and Stokke.

Maxwell, S. and Owens, T. (1991) *Commodity Aid and Counterpart Funds in Africa,* Discussion Paper 291, IDS, University of Sussex.

Mellor, J.W. and Johnston, B.F. (1984) *The world food equation: interrelations among development, employment and food consumption,* Journal of Economic Literature, Volume 22, June.

Mettrick, H. (1969) *Food Aid and Britain,* Overseas Development Institute, London.

Milk Products As Food Aid, (1969) Monthly Bulletin of Economic Statistics, Rome.

Moseley, P., Harrigan, J. and Toye, J. (1991) *Aid and Power: The World Bank and Policy Based Lending,* Vol. 1 and Vol. 2, Routledge.

Nouyrit, H. (1979) *Perspectives de developpément des principales productions agricoles Francaises en relation avec le marché mondial et remarques sur l'aide alimentaire.* In G. Ionescu, op.cit.

OECD (1989) *Development Co-operation: Effects and Policies of the Members of the Development Assistance Committee,* Paris.

Parotte, J.H. (1983) *The Food Aid Convention: its history and scope,* in Clay and Singer IDS Bulletin, 1983.

Persaud, B. (1986) *British agriculture and third world development.* Sixth

Agricola Conference, Wye.

Riley, B. and McClelland, D. (1990) *Enhancing the Effectiveness of Counterpart Funds in Mozambique,* IBRD/USAID Washington DC.

Robinson, C. (1989) *Hungry Farmers. World Food Response and Europe's Response.* Christian Aid.

Ruttan, V.W. (1993) *Why Food Aid?* Baltimore MD, Johns Hopkins University Press.

Schultz, T.W. (1960) "Value of US Farm Surplus to Underdeveloped Countries", *Journal of Farm Economics, Vol. 42.*

Schultz, T.W. (1980) "Effects of the International Donor Community on Farm People", *American Journal of Agricultural Economics, Vol. 62, no.2.*

Shaw, J. and Clay, E.J. (1993) *World Food Aid,* WFP and Heinemann, London.

Shefrin, F. (1965) "The World Food Program - an International Experiment in the Use of Food Aid to Developing Countries", *Economic Analist,* vol. 34, Ottawa.

Shonefield A. (1965) *Modern Capitalism,* Oxford University Press.

Singer, H.W. (1965) "Project or Plan Aid", *Economic Journal,* Vol.75.

Singer, H.W. (1978) *Food Aid Policies and Programmes. A Survey of Studies of Food Aid,* WFP/CFA, Rome.

Singer, H.W. (1991) *Food Aid and structural Adjustment in sub-Sahara Africa,* in Clay and Stokke

Singer, H.W., Wood, S. and Jennings, T. (1987) *Food aid, the challenge and the opportunity.* Oxford UniversityPress.

Sinha, R.P. (1976) "World Food Security", *Journal of Agricultural Economics.*

Srivastava, U.K. (1969) PL 480 Counterpart Funds and Inflation: Myth and Reality, *Asian Economic Review,* vol. 11.

Srivastava, U.K. (1972) *Impact of PL 480 on India's Money Supply and External Debt Service Obligations: a look ahead,* Ames, USA. CARD Report, Iowa State University, no.44.

Stevens, C. (1977) *"Food Aid: More Sinned Against than sinning?"* Overseas Development Institute Review 2, vol. 15.

Sturgess, I.M. (1995) *Food Security, self-sufficiency and protectionism in the Developed World,* Agricultural Economics Unit, University of Cambridge.

130

Surface, F.M. and Bland, R.L. (1932) *American Food in the World War and Reconstruction period,* Stanford University Press.

Talbot, R.B. (1979) *The European Community's food aid programme.* Food Policy, November.

Talbot, R.B. (1990) *The Four World Food Agencies in Rome,* Iowa State University Press, Ames.

Tarp Finn (1993) *Stabilisation and Structural Adjustment,* Routledge.

Taylor, J. and Roberts, G.K. (1979) *The policy of food aid (conclusions),* in G. Ionescu. op.cit.

Terhal, P. and Doornbos, M. (1983) *Operation Flood, development and commercialization,* Food Policy, August.

The Times (1987) "EEC: Food aid is catalogue of disaster" say Auditors. September 3.

Thomson, A.M. (1983) *Egypt, Food Security and food aid,* Food Policy, August.

Tracy, M. and Hodac, I. (ed) (1979) *Prospects For Agriculture in the European Economic Community,* Bruges.

Tsoukalis, L. (1993) *The New European Economy, the Politics and economics of integration* (2nd edition), Oxford University Press.

USDA (1982) *World food aid needs and availability.* Washington.

Van Meerhaeghe, M.A.G. (1971) *International Economic Institutions* (second edition), Longman, London.

Wallerstein, M. (1980) *Food for peace, food for war: United States Food Aid in a global context,* Cambridge, Mass.

Wightman, D.R. (1968) *Food Aid and Economic Development.* Carnegie Endowment for International Peace. No.567, Washington.

Williams, J.C. and Wright, B.D. (1991) *Storage and Commodity markets,* Cambridge University Press.

World Bank (1986) *World Development Report,* Washington.

World Food Programme/Government of Netherlands (1983) *Report of the World Food Programme,* Government of Netherlands Seminar on Food Aid, WFP, Rome.

World Food Programme/African Development Bank (1986) *Food Aid for Development in Sub-Sahara Africa,* Abidjan.